THE NEW TEMPLE SHAKESPEARE

Edited by M. R. Ridley, M.A.

THE TWO GENTLEMEN OF VERONA

by William Shakespeare

London: J. M. DENT & SONS LTD.
New York: E. P. DUTTON & CO. INC.

Editor's General Note

The Text. The editor has kept before him the aim of presenting to the modern reader the nearest possible approximation to what Shakespeare actually wrote. The text is therefore conservative, and is based on the earliest reliable printed text. But to avoid distraction (*a*) the spelling is modernised, and (*b*) a limited number of universally accepted emendations is admitted without comment. Where a Quarto text exists as well as the First Folio the passages which occur only in the Quarto are enclosed in square brackets [ ] and those which occur only in the Folio in brace brackets { }.

Scene Division. The rapid continuity of the Elizabethan curtainless production is lost by the 'traditional' scene divisions. Where there is an essential difference of place these scene divisions are retained. Where on the other hand the change of place is insignificant the scene division is indicated only by a space on the page. For ease of reference, however, the 'traditional' division is retained at the head of the page and in line numbering.

Notes. Passages on which there are notes are indicated by a † in the margin.

Punctuation adheres more closely than has been usual to the 'Elizabethan' punctuation of the early texts. It is often therefore more indicative of the way in which the lines were to be delivered than of their syntactical construction.

Glossaries are arranged on a somewhat novel principle, not alphabetically, but in the order in which the words or phrases occur. The editor is much indebted to Mr J. N. Bryson for his collaboration in the preparation of the glossaries.

Preface

The Text. The play was printed for the first time, so far as we know, in the First Folio in 1623. Apart from some carelessness in punctuation the text is, at any rate superficially, an excellent one; it contains, that is, very few of those obviously corrupt passages which must be emended before they will yield even tolerable sense. But that very clarity rather suggests that the copy used was not author's MS., but a clearly written transcript, in which any obscurities had been tidied up. And a transcript, particularly a transcript of the acting version of a play, may be at some distance from the play as it left the author's hands. It is likely to give the play as it cut for presentation, and if it is made by someone who is familiar with the play on the boards, it is also likely to incorporate actors' errors, and possibly their gags. But if F had been set from a direct transcript of the acting version (and a fortiori if it had been set from the author's MS.) it is improbable, almost to impossibility, that it would have exhibited that oddity in its stage-directions which (in common with two or three other plays) it does in fact exhibit. Briefly, the play as it stands in F could not possibly be handed over to a company for production until some-one had gone carefully through it and inserted all the necessary entries and exits, to say nothing of directions for any necessary business. There are only four exits indicated except at the ends of scenes, and there are no entries at all except at the beginnings of scenes, where all the actors who are to appear in that particular scene are blocked together. This peculiarity leads the New Cambridge editors to apply to the play their theory of 'assembled texts,' texts, that is, which in the absence (for whatever reason) of

vii

a complete MS. were pieced together from the individual actors' parts with the aid of the 'plot,' which was a sheet giving for each scene of the play the names of the characters playing in it in the order of their appearance. Now this theory (like many other theories) is much more plausible at first glance than it becomes under detailed examination. The moment that we stop talking vaguely about piecing together actors' parts, and begin to visualise, as we should, the exact operation that the unhappy piecer had to conduct with this dramatic humpty-dumpty, there being nothing to help him in fitting together the various bits of the half-dozen parts in front of him except brief cues and the 'plot,' then we begin to wonder why it is that there seem no signs of the kind of error that such a method of reconstructing a play must almost inevitably produce. But because a theory is not as plausible as one could wish, it does not therefore follow that it is impossible, and even Sir Edmund Chambers, who is highly suspicious of it, and clearly outlines the objections in his *William Shakespeare* (i. 153-55), yet admits that 'perhaps the case for it is stronger in the *Two Gentlemen* than elsewhere.' I am at best lukewarm about the theory, but I find it impossible to deny that in this instance it seems to explain the facts; and one cannot pretend that, as happens with some theories, it creates more difficulties than it solves. If the mechanics of the thing are possible, a text thus assembled would present the peculiarities presented by the Folio; and as to the mechanics it should be noticed that the bulk of the action of the play is conducted with not more than three speaking characters on the stage at one time, and much of it with only two, so that the task of the assembler is correspondingly easier and less liable to serious error.

The New Cambridge editors also see the hand of an 'adapter,' who shortened the play for presentation, though at the same time, oddly enough, and inconsistently with his supposed purpose, he is assumed to have created the character of Speed. The advantage of this 'adapter' is, of course, that we can shift on to his shadowy shoulders anything of which we want to relieve Shakespeare, notably Speed, and the tasteless clumsiness of the last scene. The play is indeed unusually short, and I have little doubt that what we have is an acting version, cut as *Hamlet* was cut, though much less skilfully; but the evidence which is adduced for the existence of anyone who can in any proper sense be called an adapter, whose operations included transposition and insertion as well as straightforward cutting, seems to me very dubious. Here, for example, are two instances of the literary evidence, which, we are told, ' is so strong as to be overwhelming.' At II. iv. 192-94, F (so it is stated, but see note on the passage) reads :

> *It is mine. or Valentines praise?*
> *Her true perfection, or my false transgression?*
> *That makes me reasonlesse, to reason thus?*

The first line, we are told, is 'hopeless'; if it is, the occasions for despair in reading Shakespeare are deplorably numerous, and the New Cambridge editors themselves are not in other places, where despair is less helpful to an argument, so ready to throw up the sponge. They go on : 'the F period, "It is" and the absolutely unmetrical character of the line as it stands render legitimate emendation impossible. We are, therefore, forced to the conclusion that the text has been tampered with at this point, in order to shorten the soliloquy.' This is a staggering conclusion; it means simply that whenever in reading a Shakespearean text we come upon a line of unmetrical nonsense we must not try to emend;

we are not only justified in concluding, but forced to conclude, that the text at that point has been tampered with by cutting. (We are not, it will be remembered, examining the passage in front of us with the existence of the adapter already proved; if we were, we might reasonably enough suspect him of being responsible for the muddle; we are invited to examine the passage as part of the overwhelming evidence that the adapter existed at all.) The passage is further commented on in the Notes. Again, V. iv. 88-90:

Jul. *O good sir, my master charg'd me to deliver a ring to Madam Silvia : which (out of my neglect) was never done.*

' The occurrence of an isolated prose speech in the middle of a verse scene raises suspicions. But suspicion becomes certainty when it is observed that

> *Which, out of my neglect, was never done*

is a line of verse. In other words, the adapter has here tampered with the text, using, however, a scrap of Shakespeare's original to patch the rent.' Now, in the first place the prose speech is not ' isolated'; Julia's swoon seems for the moment to deprive all the characters of their facility in versifying (though this no doubt may also be due to the adapter). In the second place, what sort of tampering, and for what end, is the adapter supposed to have done? All that is wanted is a mention of the ring to introduce the offer of the other ring, and it is hardly reasonable to suppose that Shakespeare took longer about it than the supposed adapter. In the third place, this evidence of ' verse-fossils,' of which the New Cambridge editors are peculiarly fond, seems to me, as I have tried to show in the Preface to *As You Like It*, singularly untrustworthy. Ten minutes' research in this play yielded the following :

(Launce).   *He is a stone, a very pebble-stone,*
     (*and*) *Has no more pity in him than a dog.*   II. iii. 10-11.

(Valentine). *Yourself, sweet lady, for you gave the fire.*   II. iv. 34.

(Launce).   *I care not, though he burn himself in love.*   II. v. 44.

                           I am but
    A fool, look you ; and yet I have the wit
    To think my master is a kind of knave :
    But that's all one, if he be but one knave.
                       III. i. 261-63.

There is then the evidence of supposedly curtailed scenes, particularly II. ii. and V. iii. Here ' we are presented with what are apparently nothing but the conclusions of longer scenes in the original, the adapter attempting to conceal his traces by writing a few lines of prose as an introduction.' On this there are two observations to be made, first, that it is surely perfectly characteristic of Shakespeare to have a brief scene in which the characters enter already engaged in conversation ; and second, that an adapter who attempted to conceal his traces by a process which, the argument itself claims, only advertises them, must have been no better than an ass. However, for the details of the argument and for further possible evidence of this adapter's existence the reader must be referred to the New Cambridge edition. Here I will only repeat that I think it more than likely that the play as we have it is a somewhat cut version, though I do not think that the cutting can be proved, nor the position of the excisions determined with more than some degree of probability ; that I am perfectly ready to believe that Shakespeare could be careless about time sequence, and about geography, and was capable of creating Speed and of writing indifferent verse ; and that the argument for the existence of the 'adapter' seems to me mostly argument in a circle, even though in the course of it our attention is most usefully drawn to certain features in the play.

But there is one scene in the play of which one must say something. The last scene of all, one may hope, has never satisfied any critic or reader yet. The focus of the trouble is, of course, the 'surrender' line of Valentine, *All that was mine in Silvia I give thee.* It is not merely that it carries the strained loyalty of friendship (a commonplace in the Elizabethan age) to a pitch which even to the Elizabethans, one would think, must be a trifle absurd, while to us it is revolting; the trouble is deeper than that; the surrender in itself, and indeed this whole section of the scene, is hopelessly undramatic. Valentine has been shown to us as the devoted, and not only devoted but determined, young lover. And that he, when the girl for whom he has ventured and endured so much is suddenly restored to him, should hand her over to the false friend, who has just tried to ravish her, with as hurried and casual a nonchalance as though she were a hackneyed mistress whom he was glad to discard, this is not only a wound to our sensibilities, but an outrage to common sense. If this was to be the climax Valentine should have been otherwise drawn; if the picture of Valentine is true, this climax is ridiculous. Further, what happens to Silvia? After her *O heaven* in l. 59 she has not another word to say for the rest of the play, and what is even more remarkable, though her presence is implied, Valentine does not address a word to her, not so much as *My gracious silence*. It is Julia who suddenly becomes the centre of attention, while apparently Silvia stands quietly by and watches herself bandied about between the two men, and restored to Valentine—if indeed she has any further use for him—only because Proteus abruptly finds all that he found in her more fresh in Julia. The real criticism of this scene as it stands is the practical difficulties in which the producer finds himself entangled when he tries to put it on the stage.

It just will not work. The comedy has no doubt been light and artificial, but just for that reason its conclusion, though it may also be artificial, must be neat and not botched. Shakespeare has some hurried play endings, but though we may feel dissatisfied with, for example, the pairings off at the end of *As You Like It* and *Measure for Measure*, at least they are theatrically slick and neat. If the ending of the *Two Gentlemen* is Shakespeare, all one can do is to regret it and say that he still had much to learn. But I think that here the New Cambridge editors make out a better case than elsewhere for some tinkering. I know that there is a danger of both finding and accepting evidence too easily when it will enable us to clear Shakespeare of such bad craftsmanship, but I think that any reader who will read the scene with suspicion will probably feel with the New Cambridge editors that it falls into three sections of oddly different quality and 'feel'; first the Valentine-Proteus-Silvia section, down to Valentine's interruption of Proteus' attempted rape (or perhaps a few lines earlier than that); second, the Valentine-Proteus-Julia section, down to the entry of the outlaws; and third, the rest of the scene. Stylistically, the first and third sections are Shakespearean in the early manner and the second is not. One difficulty that I find in this division is that to my ear the change of style happens a few lines earlier than it should, with Proteus' *And love you gainst the nature of love,—force ye.* Another is that there is a kind of neat balance in the first two sections, each concluding the speaking career of the two girls. But at the least, even if we do not assume that some of the writing is that of an 'adapter,' I think that one is vividly aware of some process of compression and inartistic dovetailing. For the detailed treatment of the scene the reader must be referred to the New Cambridge edition.

Date of Composition. There is no external evidence except Meres' mention of the play in 1598, which is of little help, since on grounds of style and temper it is clearly earlier than that. 1594-95 will probably not be far out.

Source. Probably de Montemayor's story of Felix and Felismena in his *Diana Enamorada*, either in the original, or through the medium of a translation, or of a play *Felix and Philiomena*, acted in 1585.

Duration of Action. Daniel gave seven days, with intervals. There are various awkwardnesses in the time-scheme, but I do not think that either they or the exact determination of the intervals worry the reader or spectator.

Criticism.

Hazlitt.—The style of the familiar parts of this comedy is indeed made up of conceits—low they may be for what we know, but then they are not poor, but rich ones. The scene of Launce with his dog (not that in the second, but that in the fourth act) is a perfect treat in the way of farcical drollery and invention; nor do we think Speed's manner of proving his master to be in love deficient in wit or sense, though the style may be criticised as not simple enough for the modern taste.

The tender scenes in this play, though not so highly wrought as in some others, have often much sweetness of sentiment and expression.   There is something pretty and playful in the conversation of Julia with her maid, when she shews such a disposition to coquetry about receiving the letter from Proteus; and her behaviour afterwards and her disappointment, when she finds him faithless to his vows, remind us at a distance of Imogen's tender constancy.

Swinburne.[1]—'. . . in the *Two Gentlemen of Verona* rhyme has fallen seemingly into abeyance, and there are no passages of such elegiac beauty as in the former, of such exalted eloquence as in the latter of these two plays; there is an even sweetness, a simple equality of grace in thought and language which keeps the whole poem in tune, written as it is in a subdued key of unambitious harmony.   In perfect unity and keeping the composition of this beautiful sketch may perhaps be said to mark a stage of advance, a new point of work attained, a faint but sensible change of manner, signalised by increasing firmness of hand and clearness of outline. Slight and swift in execution as it is, few and simple as are the chords here struck of character and emotion, every shade of drawing and every note of sound is at one with the whole scheme of form and music.   Here too is the first dawn of that higher and more tender humour which was never given in such perfection to any man as ultimately to Shakespeare; one touch of the by-play of Launce and his immortal dog is worth all the bright fantastic interludes of Boyet and Adriano, Costard and Holofernes; worth even half the sallies of Mercutio, and half the dancing doggerel or broad-witted prose of either Dromio.

[1] Reprinted by permission of the Publishers, W. Heinemann Ltd., from *A Study of Shakespeare.*

THE TWO GENTLEMEN OF VERONA

DRAMATIS PERSONÆ

DUKE OF MILAN, *Father to Silvia.*

VALENTINE, } *the Two Gentlemen.*
PROTEUS,

ANTONIO, *Father to Proteus.*

THURIO, *a foolish rival to Valentine.*

EGLAMOUR, *Agent for Silvia in her escape.*

HOST, *where Julia lodges.*

OUTLAWS, *with Valentine.*

SPEED, *a clownish servant to Valentine.*

LAUNCE, *the like to Proteus.*

PANTHINO, *Servant to Antonio.*

JULIA, *beloved of Proteus.*

SILVIA, *beloved of Valentine.*

LUCETTA, *waiting-woman to Julia.*

Servants, Musicians.

SCENE: *Verona; Milan; the frontiers of Mantua.*

THE TWO GENTLEMEN OF VERONA

Act First

Verona.   An open place

Enter Valentine and Proteus

Val. Cease to persuade, my loving Proteus :
 Home-keeping youth have ever homely wits.
 Were 't not affection chains thy tender days
 To the sweet glances of thy honour'd love,
 I rather would entreat thy company
 To see the wonders of the world abroad,
 Than (living dully sluggardiz'd at home)
 Wear out thy youth with shapeless idleness.
 But since thou lov'st, love still, and thrive therein,
 Even as I would, when I to love begin,   10
Pro. Wilt thou be gone ?   Sweet Valentine, adieu !
 Think on thy Proteus, when thou haply seest
 Some rare noteworthy object in thy travel :
 Wish me partaker in thy happiness,
 When thou dost meet good hap ; and in thy danger,

  (If ever danger do environ thee)
  Command thy grievance to my holy prayers,
  For I will be thy beadsman, Valentine.

Val. And on a love-book pray for my success?

Pro. Upon some book I love I'll pray for thee.   20

Val. That's on some shallow story of deep love,
  How young Leander cross'd the Hellespont.   †

Pro. That's a deep story, of a deeper love,
  For he was more than over shoes in love.

Val. 'Tis true; for you are over boots in love,
  And yet you never swum the Hellespont.

Pro. Over the boots? nay, give me not the boots.

Val. No, I will not, for it boots thee not.

Pro.   What?

Val. To be in love; where scorn is bought with groans;
  Coy looks with heart-sore sighs; one fading
    moment's mirth   30
  With twenty watchful, weary, tedious nights:
  If haply won, perhaps a hapless gain;
  If lost, why then a grievous labour won;
  However, but a folly bought with wit,
  Or else a wit by folly vanquished.

Pro. So, by your circumstance, you call me fool.

Val. So, by your circumstance, I fear you'll prove.

Pro. 'Tis love you cavil at; I am not Love.

Val. Love is your master, for he masters you :
　　And he that is so yoked by a fool,　　　　　40
　　Methinks should not be chronicled for wise.

Pro. Yet writers say, as in the sweetest bud
　　The eating canker dwells, so eating love
　　Inhabits in the finest wits of all.

Val. And writers say, as the most forward bud
　　Is eaten by the canker ere it blow,
　　Even so by love the young and tender wit
　　Is turn'd to folly, blasting in the bud,
　　Losing his verdure even in the prime,
　　And all the fair effects of future hopes.　　50
　　But wherefore waste I time to counsel thee,
　　That art a votary to fond desire ?
　　Once more adieu ! my father at the road
　　Expects my coming, there to see me shipp'd.

Pro. And thither will I bring thee, Valentine.

Val. Sweet Proteus, no ; now let us take our leave.
　　To Milan let me hear from thee by letters
　　Of thy success in love, and what news else
　　Betideth here in absence of thy friend ;
　　And I likewise will visit thee with mine.　　60

Pro. All happiness bechance to thee in Milan !

Val. As much to you at home ! and so, farewell.　　*Exit*

Pro. He after honour hunts, I after love :

3

He leaves his friends, to dignify them more;
I leave myself, my friends, and all, for love.
Thou, Julia, thou hast metamorphis'd me,
Made me neglect my studies, lose my time;
War with good counsel; set the world at nought;
Made wit with musing weak; heart sick with thought.

Enter Speed

Sp. Sir Proteus, save you! Saw you my master?   70
Pro. But now he parted hence to embark for Milan.
Sp. Twenty to one, then, he is shipp'd already,   †
  And I have play'd the sheep in losing him.
Pro. Indeed, a sheep doth very often stray,
  An if the shepherd be awhile away.
Sp. You conclude that my master is a shepherd, then,
  and I a sheep?
Pro. I do.
Sp. Why then, my horns are his horns, whether I wake
  or sleep.   80
Pro. A silly answer, and fitting well a sheep.
Sp. This proves me still a sheep.
Pro. True; and thy master a shepherd.
Sp. Nay, that I can deny by a circumstance.
Pro. It shall go hard but I 'll prove it by another.
Sp. The shepherd seeks the sheep, and not the sheep the

4

shepherd ; but I seek my master, and my master
seeks me not : therefore I am no sheep.

Pro. The sheep for fodder follow the shepherd, the shepherd for food follows not the sheep : thou for 90
wages followest thy master, thy master for wages
follows not thee : therefore thou art a sheep.

Sp. Such another proof will make me cry ' baa.'

Pro. But, dost thou hear ? gav'st thou my letter to Julia ?

Sp. Ay, sir : I (a lost mutton) gave your letter to her
(a lac'd mutton) and she (a lac'd mutton) gave me
(a lost mutton) nothing for my labour.

Pro. Here 's too small a pasture for such store of muttons.

Sp. If the ground be overcharg'd, you were best stick her.

Pro. Nay, in that you are astray ; 'twere best pound you. 100

Sp. Nay, sir, less than a pound shall serve me for carrying
your letter.

Pro. You mistake ; I mean the pound,—a pinfold.

Sp. From a pound to a pin ? fold it over and over,
'Tis threefold too little for carrying a letter to your
lover.

Pro. But what said she ?

Sp. (*first nodding*) Ay.

Pro. Nod—Ay—why, that 's noddy.

Sp. You mistook, sir ; I say she did nod : and you ask
me if she did nod, and I say, ' Ay.' 110

Pro. And that set together is noddy.

Sp. Now you have taken the pains to set it together, take it for your pains.

Pro. No no, you shall have it for bearing the letter.

Sp. Well, I perceive I must be fain to bear with you.

Pro. Why, sir, how do you bear with me?

Sp. Marry, sir, the letter, very orderly, having nothing but the word 'noddy' for my pains.

Pro. Beshrew me, but you have a quick wit.

Sp. And yet it cannot overtake your slow purse.   120

Pro. Come, come, open the matter in brief: what said she?

Sp. Open your purse, that the money and the matter may be both at once delivered.

Pro. Well, sir; here is for your pains; what said she?

Sp. Truly, sir, I think you 'll hardly win her.

Pro. Why? couldst thou perceive so much from her?

Sp. Sir, I could perceive nothing at all from her; no, not so much as a ducat for delivering your letter: and being so hard to me that brought your mind, I fear she 'll prove as hard to you in telling your mind.   130 Give her no token but stones, for she 's as hard as steel.

Pro. What said she? nothing?

Sp. No, not so much as 'Take this for thy pains.' To testify your bounty, I thank you, you have testerned

6

me ; in requital whereof, henceforth, carry your
letters yourself : and so, sir, I 'll commend you to
my master.

Pro. Go, go, be gone, to save your ship from wreck,
Which cannot perish having thee aboard,   140
Being destin'd to a drier death on shore.   *Exit Speed* †
I must go send some better messenger :
I fear my Julia would not deign my lines,
Receiving them from such a worthless post.   *Exit*

SCENE II

The same.   Garden of Julia's house

Enter Julia and Lucetta

Jul. But say, Lucetta, now we are alone,
Wouldst thou then counsel me to fall in love ?

Luc. Ay, madam ; so you stumble not unheedfully.

Jul. Of all the fair resort of gentlemen
That every day with parle encounter me,
In thy opinion which is worthiest love ?

Luc. Please you repeat their names, I 'll show my mind   †
According to my shallow simple skill.

Jul. What think'st thou of the fair Sir Eglamour ?

Luc. As of a knight well-spoken, neat and fine ;   10

7

But were I you, he never should be mine.

Jul. What think'st thou of the rich Mercatio?

Luc. Well of his wealth; but of himself, so so.

Jul. What think'st thou of the gentle Proteus?

Luc. Lord, Lord! to see what folly reigns in us!

Jul. How now? what means this passion at his name?

Luc. Pardon, dear madam, 'tis a passing shame
That I (unworthy body as I am)
Should censure thus on lovely gentlemen.

Jul. Why not on Proteus, as of all the rest? 20

Luc. Then thus,—of many good I think him best.

Jul. Your reason?

Luc. I have no other but a woman's reason;
I think him so, because I think him so.

Jul. And wouldst thou have me cast my love on him?

Luc. Ay, if you thought your love not cast away.

Jul. Why he, of all the rest, hath never mov'd me.

Luc. Yet he, of all the rest, I think best loves ye.

Jul. His little speaking shows his love but small.

Luc. Fire that's closest kept burns most of all. 30

Jul. They do not love, that do not show their love.

Luc. O, they love least that let men know their love.

Jul. I would I knew his mind.

Luc. Peruse this paper, madam.

Jul. ' To Julia.'—Say, from whom?

Luc. That the contents will show.

Jul. Say, say, who gave it thee ?

Luc. Sir Valentine's page ; and sent, I think, from Proteus.
    He would have given it you ; but I, being in the way,
    Did in your name receive it : pardon the fault, I pray. 40

Jul. Now, by my modesty, a goodly broker ?
    Dare you presume to harbour wanton lines ?
    To whisper and conspire against my youth ?
    Now trust me, 'tis an office of great worth,
    And you an officer fit for the place,
    There ; take the paper : see it be return'd,
    Or else return no more into my sight.

Luc. To plead for love deserves more fee than hate.

Jul. Will ye be gone ?

Luc.   That you may ruminate.   *Exit*

Jul. And yet I would I had o'erlook'd the letter ;   50
    It were a shame to call her back again,
    And pray her to a fault for which I chid her.
    What fool is she, that knows I am a maid,
    And would not force the letter to my view !
    Since maids, in modesty, say ' no ' to that
    Which they would have the profferer construe ' ay.'
    Fie, fie ; how wayward is this foolish love,
    That, like a testy babe, will scratch the nurse,
    And presently, all humbled, kiss the rod !

9

60

How churlishly I chid Lucetta hence,
When willingly I would have had her here !
How angerly I taught my brow to frown,
When inward joy enforc'd my heart to smile !
My penance is, to call Lucetta back,
And ask remission for my folly past.
What, ho ! Lucetta !

Re-enter Lucetta

Luc.   What would your ladyship ?
Jul. Is 't near dinner-time ?
Luc.   I would it were ;
That you might kill your stomach on your meat,
And not upon your maid.
Jul. What is 't that you took up so gingerly ?   70
Luc. Nothing.
Jul. Why didst thou stoop, then ?
Luc. To take a paper up that I let fall.
Jul. And is that paper nothing ?
Luc. Nothing concerning me.
Jul. Then let it lie, for those that it concerns.
Luc. Madam, it will not lie where it concerns,
Unless it have a false interpreter.
Jul. Some love of yours hath writ to you in rhyme.
Luc. That I might sing it, madam, to a tune :   †
Give me a note : your ladyship can set.   81

10

Jul. As little by such toys as may be possible :
　　Best sing it to the tune of ' Light o' love.'　　　　†

Luc. It is too heavy for so light a tune.

Jul. Heavy ? belike it hath some burden then ?

Luc. Ay ; and melodious were it, would you sing it.

Jul. And why not you ?

Luc. 　　　　　　　I cannot reach so high.

Jul. Let 's see your song.　How now, minion ?

Luc. Keep tune there still ; so you will sing it out :
　　And yet methinks I do not like this tune.　　　　90

Jul. You do not ?

Luc. 　　　　　No, madam, 'tis too sharp.

Jul. You, minion, are too saucy.

Luc. Nay, now you are too flat,
　　And mar the concord with too harsh a descant :
　　There wanteth but a mean to fill your song.

Jul. The mean is drown'd with your unruly bass.

Luc. Indeed, I bid the base for Proteus.

Jul. This babble shall not henceforth trouble me.　　†
　　Here is a coil with protestation !　　　*Tears the letter*
　　Go get you gone ; and let the papers lie :　　　100
　　You would be fingering them, to anger me.

Luc. She makes it strange, but she would be best pleas'd
　　To be so anger'd with another letter.　　　*Exit*

Jul. Nay, would I were so anger'd with the same !

11

O hateful hands, to tear such loving words !
Injurious wasps, to feed on such sweet honey,
And kill the bees, that yield it, with your stings !
I 'll kiss each several paper, for amends.
Look, here is writ ' kind Julia.' Unkind Julia !
As in revenge of thy ingratitude, 110
I throw thy name against the bruising stones,
Trampling contemptuously on thy disdain.
And here is writ ' love-wounded Proteus.'
Poor wounded name ! my bosom, as a bed,
Shall lodge thee till thy wound be throughly heal'd ;
And thus I search it with a sovereign kiss.
But twice, or thrice, was ' Proteus ' written down.
Be calm, good wind, blow not a word away,
Till I have found each letter in the letter,
Except mine own name : that some whirlwind bear 120
Unto a ragged, fearful, hanging rock,
And throw it thence into the raging sea !
Lo, here in one line is his name twice writ,
' Poor forlorn Proteus, passionate Proteus,
To the sweet Julia ' :—that I 'll tear away.—
And yet I will not, sith so prettily
He couples it to his complaining names.
Thus will I fold them, one upon another :
Now kiss, embrace, contend, do what you will.

Re-enter Lucetta

Luc. Madam,   130
    Dinner is ready, and your father stays.

Jul. Well, let us go.

Luc. What, shall these papers lie, like tell-tales here?

Jul. If you respect them, best to take them up.

Luc. Nay, I was taken up for laying them down:
    Yet here they shall not lie, for catching cold.

Jul. I see you have a month's mind to them.   †

Luc. Ay, madam, you may say what sights you see;
    I see things too, although you judge I wink.

Jul. Come, come, will't please you go?   *Exeunt* 140

SCENE III

The same.   Antonio's house

Enter Antonio and Panthino

Ant. Tell me, Panthino, what sad talk was that
    Wherewith my brother held you in the cloister?

Pan. 'Twas of his nephew Proteus, your son.

Ant. Why, what of him?

Pan.   He wonder'd that your lordship
    Would suffer him to spend his youth at home,
    While other men, of slender reputation,

13

Put forth their sons, to seek preferment out :
Some to the wars, to try their fortune there ;
Some to discover islands far away ;
Some to the studious universities.   10
For any, or for all these exercises,
He said that Proteus, your son, was meet ;
And did request me to importune you
To let him spend his time no more at home ;
Which would be great impeachment to his age,
In having known no travel in his youth.

Ant. Nor need'st thou much importune me to that
Whereon this month I have been hammering.
I have consider'd well, his loss of time,
And how he cannot be a perfect man,   20
Not being tried, and tutor'd in the world :
Experience is by industry achiev'd,
And perfected by the swift course of time.
Then, tell me, whither were I best to send him ?

Pan. I think your lordship is not ignorant
How his companion, youthful Valentine,
Attends the emperor in his royal court.

Ant. I know it well.

Pan. 'Twere good, I think, your lordship sent him thither :
There shall he practise tilts and tournaments,   30
Hear sweet discourse, converse with noblemen,

14

And be in eye of every exercise
Worthy of his youth and nobleness of birth.

Ant. I like thy counsel ; well hast thou advis'd :
And that thou mayst perceive how well I like it
The execution of it shall make known.
Even with the speediest expedition
I will dispatch him to the emperor's court.

Pan. To-morrow, may it please you, Don Alphonso,
With other gentlemen of good esteem,   40
Are journeying to salute the emperor,
And to commend their service to his will.

Ant. Good company ; with them shall Proteus go :
And in good time ! now will we break with him.

Enter Proteus

Pro. Sweet love, sweet lines, sweet life !
Here is her hand, the agent of her heart ;
Here is her oath for love, her honour's pawn ;
O, that our fathers would applaud our loves,
To seal our happiness with their consents !
O heavenly Julia !   50

Ant. How now ? what letter are you reading there ?

Pro. May 't please your lordship, 'tis a word or two
Of commendations sent from Valentine,
Deliver'd by a friend that came from him.

Ant. Lend me the letter ; let me see what news.

Pro. There is no news, my lord, but that he writes
　　How happily he lives, how well belov'd,
　　And daily graced by the emperor ;
　　Wishing me with him, partner of his fortune.
Ant. And how stand you affected to his wish ?　　60
Pro. As one relying on your lordship's will,
　　And not depending on his friendly wish.
Ant. My will is something sorted with his wish.
　　Muse not that I thus suddenly proceed ;
　　For what I will, I will, and there an end.
　　I am resolv'd that thou shalt spend some time
　　With Valentinus, in the emperor's court :
　　What maintenance he from his friends receives,
　　Like exhibition thou shalt have from me ;
　　To-morrow be in readiness to go :　　70
　　Excuse it not, for I am peremptory.
Pro. My lord, I cannot be so soon provided ;
　　Please you deliberate a day or two.
Ant. Look, what thou want'st shall be sent after thee :
　　No more of stay ! to-morrow thou must go ;
　　Come on, Panthino : you shall be employ'd
　　To hasten on his expedition.　　*Exeunt Ant. and Pan.*
Pro. Thus have I shunn'd the fire, for fear of burning,
　　And drench'd me in the sea, where I am drown'd.
　　I fear'd to show my father Julia's letter,　　80

Lest he should take exceptions to my love,
And with the vantage of mine own excuse
Hath he excepted most against my love.
O, how this spring of love resembleth
    The uncertain glory of an April day,
Which now shows all the beauty of the sun,
    And by and by a cloud takes all away !

Re-enter Panthino

Pan. Sir Proteus, your father calls for you,
    He is in haste, therefore, I pray you, go.
Pro. Why, this it is : my heart accords thereto,   90
    And yet a thousand times it answers ' no.'   *Exeunt*

Act Second

SCENE I

Milan.   The Duke's palace

Enter Valentine and Speed

Sp. Sir, your glove.
Val.   Not mine ; my gloves are on.
Sp. Why, then, this may be yours ; for this is but one.

Val. Ha ! let me see : ay, give it me, it 's mine :
  Sweet ornament that decks a thing divine !
  Ah, Silvia, Silvia !

Sp. Madam Silvia ! Madam Silvia !

Val. How now, sirrah ?

Sp. She is not within hearing, sir.

Val. Why, sir, who bade you call her ?

Sp. Your worship, sir, or else I mistook.   10

Val. Well, you 'll still be too forward.

Sp. And yet I was last chidden for being too slow.

Val. Go to, sir, tell me, do you know Madam Silvia ?

Sp. She that your worship loves ?

Val. Why, how know you that I am in love ?

Sp. Marry, by these special marks : first, you have learn'd
  (like Sir Proteus) to wreathe your arms like a mal-
  content ; to relish a love-song, like a robin-redbreast ;
  to walk alone like one that had the pestilence ; to sigh,
  like a school-boy that had lost his A B C ; to weep 20
  like a young wench that had buried her grandam ; to
  fast, like one that takes diet ; to watch, like one that
  fears robbing ; to speak puling, like a beggar at
  Hallowmas. You were wont, when you laughed,
  to crow like a cock ; when you walk'd, to walk like
  one of the lions ; when you fasted, it was presently
  after dinner ; when you look'd sadly, it was for want

of money : and now you are metamorphis'd with a
mistress, that, when I look on you, I can hardly think
you my master.   30

Val. Are all these things perceiv'd in me ?

Sp. They are all perceiv'd without ye.

Val. Without me ? they cannot.

Sp. Without you ? nay, that 's certain ; for without
you were so simple, none else would : but you are †
so without these follies, that these follies are within
you, and shine through you like the water in an
urinal ; that not an eye that sees you but is a physician
to comment on your malady.

Val. But tell me ; dost thou know my lady Silvia ?   40

Sp. She that you gaze on so, as she sits at supper ?

Val. Hast thou observ'd that ? even she I mean.

Sp. Why, sir, I know her not.

Val. Dost thou know her by my gazing on her, and yet
know'st her not ?

Sp. Is she not hard-favour'd, sir ?

Val. Not so fair, boy, as well-favour'd.

Sp. Sir, I know that well enough.

Val. What dost thou know ?

Sp. That she is not so fair as (of you) well favour'd.   50

Val. I mean that her beauty is exquisite, but her favour
infinite.

Sp. That's because the one is painted, and the other out of all count.

Val. How painted ? and how out of count ?

Sp. Marry, sir, so painted to make her fair, that no man counts of her beauty.

Val. How esteem'st thou me ? I account of her beauty.

Sp. You never saw her since she was deform'd.

Val. How long hath she been deform'd ?   60

Sp. Ever since you lov'd her.

Val. I have lov'd her ever since I saw her, and still I see her beautiful.

Sp. If you love her, you cannot see her.

Val. Why ?

Sp. Because Love is blind. O, that you had mine eyes, or your own eyes had the lights they were wont to have, when you chid at Sir Proteus, for going ungarter'd !

Val. What should I see then ?   70

Sp. Your own present folly, and her passing deformity : for he, being in love, could not see to garter his hose ; and you, being in love, cannot see to put on †
your hose.

Val. Belike, boy, then you are in love, for last morning you could not see to wipe my shoes.

Sp. True, sir ; I was in love with my bed : I thank you,

you swing'd me for my love, which makes me the
bolder to chide you for yours.

Val. In conclusion, I stand affected to her.   80

Sp. I would you were set, so your affection would cease.

Val. Last night she enjoin'd me to write some lines to
one she loves.

Sp. And have you ?

Val. I have.

Sp. Are they not lamely writ ?

Val. No, boy, but as well as I can do them.   Peace, here
she comes.

Sp. (*aside*) O excellent motion !   O exceeding puppet !
Now will he interpret to her.   90

Enter Silvia

Val. Madam and mistress, a thousand good-morrows.

Sp. (*aside*) O, give ye good even ! here 's a million of
manners.

Sil. Sir Valentine and servant, to you two thousand.

Sp. (*aside*) He should give her interest, and she gives it
him.

Val. As you enjoin'd me, I have writ your letter
Unto the secret nameless friend of yours ;
Which I was much unwilling to proceed in,
But for my duty to your ladyship.   100

Sil. I thank you, gentle servant, 'tis very clerkly done.

Val. Now trust me, madam, it came hardly off;
 For, being ignorant to whom it goes,
 I writ at random, very doubtfully.

Sil. Perchance you think too much of so much pains?

Val. No, madam; so it stead you, I will write,
 Please you command a thousand times as much;
 And yet—

Sil. A pretty period! Well, I guess the sequel;
 And yet I will not name it;—and yet I care not;— 110
 And yet, take this again:—and yet I thank you;
 Meaning henceforth to trouble you no more.

Sp. (*aside*) 'And yet,' you will; 'and yet,' another yet.

Val. What means your ladyship? do you not like it?

Sil. Yes, yes: the lines are very quaintly writ;
 But, since unwillingly, take them again.
 Nay, take them.

Val. Madam, they are for you.

Sil. Ay, ay: you writ them, sir, at my request,
 But I will none of them; they are for you; 120
 I would have had them writ more movingly.

Val. Please you, I'll write your ladyship another.

Sil. And when it's writ, for my sake read it over,
 And if it please you, so; if not, why, so.

Val. If it please me, madam, what then?

Sil. Why, if it please you, take it for your labour:

And so, good morrow, servant.   *Exit*

Sp. O jest unseen ; inscrutable ; invisible,
As a nose on a man's face, or a weathercock on a steeple !
My master sues to her ; and she hath taught her suitor, 130
He being her pupil, to become her tutor.
O excellent device ! was there ever heard a better ?
That my master, being scribe, to himself should write
        the letter ?

Val. How now, sir ? what are you reasoning with yourself ?

Sp. Nay, I was rhyming : 'tis you that have the reason.

Val. To do what ?

Sp. To be a spokesman from Madam Silvia.

Val. To whom ?

Sp. To yourself : why, she woos you by a figure.   140

Val. What figure ?

Sp. By a letter, I should say.

Val. Why, she hath not writ to me.

Sp. What need she, when she hath made you write to
yourself ?   Why, do you not perceive the jest ?

Val. No, believe me.

Sp. No believing you, indeed, sir.   But did you perceive
her earnest ?

Val. She gave me none, except an angry word.

Sp. Why, she hath given you a letter.   150

23

Val. That's the letter I writ to her friend.

Sp. And that letter hath she deliver'd, and there an end.

Val. I would it were no worse.

Sp. I'll warrant you, 'tis as well :
> For often have you writ to her ; and she, in modesty,
> Or else for want of idle time, could not again reply,
> Or fearing else some messenger, that might her mind
>> discover.
> Herself hath taught her love himself to write unto
>> her lover.
> All this I speak in print, for in print I found it.
> Why muse you, sir ? 'tis dinner-time.   160

Val. I have din'd.

Sp. Ay, but hearken, sir ; though the chameleon Love
can feed on the air, I am one that am nourish'd by
my victuals ; and would fain have meat. O, be
not like your mistress ; be moved, be moved.

Exeunt

SCENE II

Verona.   Julia's house

Enter Proteus and Julia

Pro. Have patience, gentle Julia.

Jul. I must, where is no remedy.

24

Pro. When possibly I can, I will return.

Jul. If you turn not, you will return the sooner.
Keep this remembrance for thy Julia's sake.

Giving a ring

Pro. Why then we 'll make exchange ; here, take you this.

Jul. And seal the bargain with a holy kiss.

Pro. Here is my hand, for my true constancy ;
And when that hour o'erslips me in the day
Wherein I sigh not, Julia, for thy sake,   10
The next ensuing hour some foul mischance
Torment me for my love's forgetfulness !
My father stays my coming ; answer not ;
The tide is now :—nay, not thy tide of tears ;
That tide will stay me longer than I should ;
Julia, farewell !   *Exit Julia*
            What, gone without a word ?
Ay, so true love should do : it cannot speak,
For truth hath better deeds than words to grace it.

Enter Panthino

Pan. Sir Proteus, you are stay'd for.

Pro.   Go ; I come, I come.
Alas, this parting strikes poor lovers dumb.   *Exeunt*   20

25

SCENE III

The same.   A street

Enter Launce, leading a dog

Lau. Nay, 'twill be this hour ere I have done weeping ;
all the kind of the Launces have this very fault.   I
have receiv'd my proportion, like the prodigious
son, and am going with Sir Proteus to the Imperial's
court.   I think Crab my dog be the sourest-natured
dog that lives :   my mother weeping ;   my father
wailing ;   my sister crying ;   our maid howling ;   our
cat wringing her hands, and all our house in a great
perplexity, yet did not this cruel-hearted cur shed
one tear :   he is a stone, a very pebble stone, and has   10
no more pity in him than a dog : a Jew would have
wept to have seen our parting ;   why, my grandam,
having no eyes, look you, wept herself blind at my
parting.   Nay, I 'll show you the manner of it.   This
shoe is my father :   no, this left shoe is my father ;   no,
no, this left shoe is my mother :   nay, that cannot be
so neither :   yes, it is so, it is so, it hath the worser
sole.   This shoe, with the hole in it, is my mother ;
and this my father ;   a vengeance on 't, there 'tis :
now, sir, this staff is my sister ;   for, look you, she is   20

26

as white as a lily, and as small as a wand : this hat
is Nan, our maid : I am the dog : no, the dog is
himself, and I am the dog,—Oh ! the dog is me, and
I am myself ; ay, so, so.   Now come I to my father ;
Father, your blessing : now should not the shoe
speak a word for weeping : now should I kiss my
father ; well, he weeps on.   Now come I to my
mother : O, that she could speak now like a wood †
woman !   Well, I kiss her, why, there 'tis, here 's
my mother's breath up and down.   Now come I to   30
my sister ; mark the moan she makes ; now the dog
all this while sheds not a tear, nor speaks a word ;
but see how I lay the dust with my tears.

Enter Panthino

Pan. Launce, away, away ; aboard ! thy master is shipp'd,
and thou art to post after with oars.   What 's the
matter ? why weep'st thou, man ? Away, ass !
you 'll lose the tide, if you tarry any longer.

Lau. It is no matter if the tide were lost ; for it is the
unkindest tide that ever any man tied.

Pan. What 's the unkindest tide ?   40

Lau. Why, he that 's tied here, Crab, my dog.

Pan. Tut, man, I mean thou 'lt lose the flood, and, in
losing the flood, lose thy voyage, and, in losing thy
voyage, lose thy master, and, in losing thy master,

lose thy service, and, in losing thy service,—Why dost thou stop my mouth?

Lau. For fear thou shouldst lose thy tongue.

Pan. Where should I lose my tongue?

Lau. In thy tale.

Pan. In thy tail? 50

Lau. Lose the tide, and the voyage, and the master, and the service, and the tied! Why, man, if the river were dry, I am able to fill it with my tears; if the wind were down, I could drive the boat with my sighs.

Pan. Come, come away, man, I was sent to call thee.

Lau. Sir, call me what thou dar'st.

Pan. Wilt thou go?

Lau. Well, I will go. *Exeunt*

SCENE IV

Milan.   The Duke's palace

Enter Silvia, Valentine, Thurio, and Speed

Sil. Servant!

Val. Mistress?

Sp. Master, Sir Thurio frowns on you.

Val. Ay, boy, it's for love.

Sp. Not of you.

Val. Of my mistress, then.

Sp. 'Twere good you knock'd him.   *Exit*

Sil. Servant, you are sad.

Val. Indeed, madam, I seem so.

Thu. Seem you that you are not ?   10

Val. Haply I do.

Thu. So do counterfeits.

Val. So do you.

Thu. What seem I that I am not ?

Val. Wise.

Thu. What instance of the contrary ?

Val. Your folly.

Thu. And how quote you my folly ?

Val. I quote it in your jerkin.

Thu. My jerkin is a doublet.   20

Val. Well, then, I 'll double your folly.

Thu. How ?

Sil. What, angry, Sir Thurio ? do you change colour ?

Val. Give him leave, madam, he is a kind of chameleon.

Thu. That hath more mind to feed on your blood that
     live in your air.

Val. You have said, sir.

Thu. Ay, sir, and done too, for this time.

Val. I know it well, sir, you always end ere you begin.

29

Sil. A fine volley of words, gentlemen, and quickly shot 30
off.

Val. 'Tis indeed, madam, we thank the giver.

Sil. Who is that, servant?

Val. Yourself, sweet lady, for you gave the fire. Sir
Thurio borrows his wit from your ladyship's looks,
and spends what he borrows kindly in your company.

Thu. Sir, if you spend word for word with me, I shall
make your wit bankrupt.

Val. I know it well, sir; you have an exchequer of
words, and, I think, no other treasure to give your 40
followers; for it appears by their bare liveries that
they live by your bare words.

Sil. No more, gentlemen, no more:—here comes my
father.

Enter Duke

Du. Now, daughter Silvia, you are hard beset.
Sir Valentine, your father's in good health:
What say you to a letter from your friends
Of much good news?

Val.   My lord, I will be thankful
To any happy messenger from thence.

Du. Know ye Don Antonio, your countryman? 50

Val. Ay, my good lord, I know the gentleman
To be of worth, and worthy estimation,

And not without desert so well reputed.

Du. Hath he not a son?

Val. Ay, my good lord, a son that well deserves
The honour and regard of such a father.

Du. You know him well?

Val. I know him as myself; for from our infancy
We have convers'd and spent our hours together:
And though myself have been an idle truant,   60
Omitting the sweet benefit of time
To clothe mine age with angel-like perfection,
Yet hath Sir Proteus, for that's his name,
Made use and fair advantage of his days;
His years but young, but his experience old;
His head unmellow'd, but his judgement ripe;
And in a word (for far behind his worth
Comes all the praises that I now bestow)
He is complete in feature, and in mind,
With all good grace to grace a gentleman.   70

Du. Beshrew me, sir, but if he make this good,
He is as worthy for an empress' love
As meet to be an emperor's counsellor.
Well, sir, this gentleman is come to me,
With commendation from great potentates,
And here he means to spend his time awhile;
I think 'tis no unwelcome news to you.

Val. Should I have wish'd a thing, it had been he.

Du. Welcome him then according to his worth.
    Silvia, I speak to you, and you, Sir Thurio,   80
    For Valentine, I need not cite him to it ;
    I will send him hither to you presently.   *Exit*

Val. This is the gentleman I told your ladyship
    Had come along with me, but that his mistress
    Did hold his eyes, lock'd in her crystal looks.

Sil. Belike that now she hath enfranchis'd them
    Upon some other pawn for fealty.

Val. Nay, sure, I think she holds them prisoners still.

Sil. Nay then, he should be blind, and, being blind,
    How could he see his way to seek out you ?   90

Val. Why, lady, Love hath twenty pair of eyes.

Thu. They say that Love hath not an eye at all.

Val. To see such lovers, Thurio, as yourself ;
    Upon a homely object Love can wink.

Sil. Have done, have done ; here comes the gentleman.

Enter Proteus

Val. Welcome, dear Proteus !   Mistress, I beseech you,
    Confirm his welcome, with some special favour.

Sil. His worth is warrant for his welcome hither,
    If this be he you oft have wish'd to hear from.

Val. Mistress, it is : sweet lady, entertain him   100
    To be my fellow-servant to your ladyship.

Sil. Too low a mistress for so high a servant.

Pro. Not so, sweet lady, but too mean a servant
    To have a look of such a worthy mistress.

Val. Leave off discourse of disability :
    Sweet lady, entertain him for your servant.

Pro. My duty will I boast of, nothing else.

Sil. And duty never yet did want his meed :
    Servant, you are welcome to a worthless mistress.

Pro. I 'll die on him that says so but yourself.   110

Sil. That you are welcome ?

Pro.   That you are worthless.

Enter Servant

Ser. Madam, my lord your father would speak with you.

Sil. I wait upon his pleasure.   (*exit Ser.*)   Come, Sir Thurio,
    Go with me.   Once more, new servant, welcome :
    I 'll leave you to confer of home affairs ;
    When you have done, we look to hear from you.

Pro. We 'll both attend upon your ladyship.

Exeunt Silvia and Thurio

Val. Now, tell me, how do all from whence you came ?

Pro. Your friends are well, and have them much commended.

Val. And how do yours ?

Pro.   I left them all in health.   120

Val. How does your lady ? and how thrives your love ?

Pro. My tales of love were wont to weary you ;

I know you joy not in a love-discourse.

Val. Ay, Proteus, but that life is alter'd now :
I have done penance for contemning Love,
Whose high imperious thoughts have punish'd me †
With bitter fasts, with penitential groans,
With nightly tears, and daily heart-sore sighs ;
For in revenge of my contempt of love,
Love hath chas'd sleep from my enthralled eyes,   130
And made them watchers of mine own heart's sorrow.
O gentle Proteus, Love 's a mighty lord,
And hath so humbled me, as I confess
There is no woe to his correction,
Nor to his service no such joy on earth.
Now no discourse, except it be of love ;
Now can I break my fast, dine, sup, and sleep,
Upon the very naked name of love.

Pro. Enough ; I read your fortune in your eye.
Was this the idol, that you worship so ?   140

Val. Even she ; and is she not a heavenly saint ?

Pro. No ; but she is an earthly paragon.

Val. Call her divine.

Pro.   I will not flatter her.

Val. O, flatter me ; for love delights in praises.

Pro. When I was sick, you gave me bitter pills,
And I must minister the like to you.

Val. Then speak the truth by her ; if not divine,
  Yet let her be a principality,
  Sovereign to all the creatures on the earth.

Pro. Except my mistress.

Val.   Sweet, except not any,   150
  Except thou wilt except against my love.

Pro. Have I not reason to prefer mine own ?

Val. And I will help thee to prefer her too :
  She shall be dignified with this high honour,—
  To bear my lady's train, lest the base earth
  Should from her vesture chance to steal a kiss,
  And, of so great a favour growing proud,
  Disdain to root the summer-swelling flower,
  And make rough winter everlastingly.

Pro. Why, Valentine, what braggardism is this ? 160

Val. Pardon me, Proteus, all I can is nothing
  To her, whose worth makes other worthies nothing ;
  She is alone.

Pro.   Then let her alone.

Val. Not for the world : why, man, she is mine own,
  And I as rich in having such a jewel
  As twenty seas, if all their sand were pearl,
  The water nectar, and the rocks pure gold.
  Forgive me, that I do not dream on thee,
  Because thou see'st me dote upon my love.

My foolish rival, that her father likes 170
(Only for his possessions are so huge)
Is gone with her along, and I must after,
For love, thou know'st, is full of jealousy.

Pro. But she loves you?

Val. Ay, and we are betroth'd : nay more, our marriage-
hour,
With all the cunning manner of our flight,
Determin'd of; how I must climb her window,
The ladder made of cords, and all the means †
Plotted and 'greed on for my happiness.
Good Proteus, go with me to my chamber, 180
In these affairs to aid me with thy counsel.

Pro. Go on before; I shall inquire you forth :
I must unto the road, to disembark
Some necessaries that I needs must use,
And then I 'll presently attend you.

Val. Will you make haste?

Pro. I will. *Exit Valentine*
Even as one heat another heat expels,
Or as one nail by strength drives out another,
So the remembrance of my former love 190
Is by a newer object quite forgotten.
Is it mine, or Valentine's praise, †
Her true perfection, or my false transgression,

That makes me reasonless, to reason thus ?
She is fair ; and so is Julia, that I love,—
That I did love, for now my love is thaw'd ;
Which, like a waxen image 'gainst a fire,
Bears no impression of the thing it was.
Methinks my zeal to Valentine is cold,
And that I love him not as I was wont.   200
O, but I love his lady too too much !
And that 's the reason I love him so little.
How shall I dote on her with more advice,
That thus without advice begin to love her !
'Tis but her picture I have yet beheld,   †
And that hath dazzled my reason's light ;
But when I look on her perfections,
There is no reason but I shall be blind.
If I can check my erring love, I will ;
If not, to compass her I 'll use my skill.   *Exit*   210

SCENE V

The same.   A street

Enter Speed and Launce severally

Sp. Launce ! by mine honesty, welcome to Padua !
Lau. Forswear not thyself, sweet youth, for I am not

welcome. I reckon this always, that a man is never undone till he be hang'd, nor never welcome to a place till some certain shot be paid, and the hostess say ' Welcome ! '

Sp. Come on, you madcap ; I 'll to the alehouse with you presently ; where, for one shot of five pence, thou shalt have five thousand welcomes. But, sirrah, how did thy master part with Madam Julia ?   10

Lau. Marry, after they clos'd in earnest, they parted very fairly in jest.

Sp. But shall she marry him ?

Lau. No.

Sp. How, then ? shall he marry her ?

Lau. No, neither.

Sp. What, are they broken ?

Lau. No ; they are both as whole as a fish.

Sp. Why then, how stands the matter with them ?

Lau. Marry, thus ; when it stands well with him, it stands   20 well with her.

Sp. What an ass art thou ! I understand thee not.

Lau. What a block art thou, that thou canst not ! My staff understands me.

Sp. What thou sayest ?

Lau. Ay, and what I do too : look thee, I 'll but lean, and my staff understands me.

Sp. It stands under thee indeed.

Lau. Why, stand-under, and under-stand, is all one.

Sp. But tell me true, will 't be a match ? 30

Lau. Ask my dog ; if he say ay, it will ; if he say, no, it will ; if he shake his tail, and say nothing, it will.

Sp. The conclusion is then, that it will.

Lau. Thou shalt never get such a secret from me but by a parable.

Sp. 'Tis well that I get it so. But, Launce, how say'st thou, that my master is become a notable lover ?

Lau. I never knew him otherwise.

Sp. Than how ?

Lau. A notable lubber ; as thou reportest him to be. 40

Sp. Why, thou whoreson ass, thou mistak'st me.

Lau. Why fool, I meant not thee, I meant thy master.

Sp. I tell thee, my master is become a hot lover.

Lau. Why, I tell thee, I care not, though he burn himself in love. If thou wilt, go with me to the alehouse ; if not, thou art an Hebrew, a Jew, and not worth the name of Christian.

Sp. Why ?

Lau. Because thou hast not so much charity in thee as to go to the ale with a Christian. Wilt thou go ? 50

Sp. At thy service. *Exeunt*

SCENE VI

The same.   The Duke's palace

Enter Proteus

Pro. To leave my Julia : shall I be forsworn ?
To love fair Silvia : shall I be forsworn ?
To wrong my friend, I shall be much forsworn ;
And even that power, which gave me first my oath,
Provokes me to this threefold perjury ;
Love bade me swear, and Love bids me forswear ;
O sweet-suggesting Love, if thou has sinn'd,
Teach me, thy tempted subject, to excuse it !
At first I did adore a twinkling star,
But now I worship a celestial sun.   10
Unheedful vows may heedfully be broken,
And he wants wit that wants resolved will
To learn his wit to exchange the bad for better.
Fie, fie, unreverend tongue, to call her bad,
Whose sovereignty so oft thou hast preferr'd
With twenty thousand soul-confirming oaths.
I cannot leave to love ; and yet I do ;
But there I leave to love where I should love.
Julia I lose, and Valentine I lose :
If I keep them, I needs must lose myself ;   20

If I lose them, thus find I by their loss
For Valentine, myself, for Julia, Silvia.
I to myself am dearer than a friend,
For love is still most precious in itself ;
And Silvia—witness Heaven, that made her fair !—
Shows Julia but a swarthy Ethiope.
I will forget that Julia is alive,
Remembering that my love to her is dead ;
And Valentine I 'll hold an enemy,
Aiming at Silvia as a sweeter friend.   30
I cannot now prove constant to myself,
Without some treachery us'd to Valentine.
This night he meaneth with a corded ladder
To climb celestial Silvia's chamber-window ;
Myself in counsel his competitor.
Now presently I 'll give her father notice
Of their disguising and pretended flight ;
Who, all enrag'd, will banish Valentine ;
For Thurio he intends shall wed his daughter ;
But Valentine being gone, I 'll quickly cross   40
By some sly trick blunt Thurio's dull proceeding.
Love, lend me wings, to make my purpose swift,
As thou hast lent me wit, to plot this drift !   *Exit*

SCENE VII

Verona.   Julia's house

Enter Julia and Lucetta

Jul. Counsel, Lucetta ; gentle girl, assist me ;
And, even in kind love, I do conjure thee,
Who art the table wherein all my thoughts
Are visibly character'd and engrav'd,
To lesson me, and tell me some good mean,
How with my honour I may undertake
A journey to my loving Proteus.

Luc. Alas, the way is wearisome and long !

Jul. A true-devoted pilgrim is not weary
To measure kingdoms with his feeble steps,   10
Much less shall she that hath Love's wings to fly,
And when the flight is made to one so dear,
Of such divine perfection as Sir Proteus.

Luc. Better forbear till Proteus makes return.

Jul. O, know'st thou not, his looks are my soul's food ?
Pity the dearth that I have pined in,
By longing for that food so long a time.
Didst thou but know the inly touch of love,
Thou wouldst as soon go kindle fire with snow
As seek to quench the fire of love with words.   20

Luc. I do not seek to quench your love's hot fire,
　　But qualify the fire's extreme rage,
　　Lest it should burn above the bounds of reason.

Jul. The more thou damm'st it up, the more it burns :
　　The current that with gentle murmur glides,
　　Thou know'st, being stopp'd, impatiently doth rage :
　　But when his fair course is not hindered,
　　He makes sweet music with the enamell'd stones,
　　Giving a gentle kiss to every sedge
　　He overtaketh in his pilgrimage ;　　　　　　　　30
　　And so by many winding nooks he strays,
　　With willing sport, to the wild ocean.　　　　　　†
　　Then let me go, and hinder not my course :
　　I 'll be as patient as the gentle stream,
　　And make a pastime of each weary step,
　　Till the last step have brought me to my love ;
　　And there I 'll rest, as after much turmoil
　　A blessed soul doth in Elysium.

Luc. But in what habit will you go along ?

Jul. Not like a woman, for I would prevent　　　　　40
　　The loose encounters of lascivious men :
　　Gentle Lucetta, fit me with such weeds
　　As may beseem some well-reputed page.

Luc. Why then your ladyship must cut your hair.

Jul. No, girl, I 'll knit it up in silken strings

With twenty odd-conceited true-love knots :
To be fantastic may become a youth
Of greater time than I shall show to be.

Luc. What fashion, madam, shall I make your breeches ?   50

Jul. That fits as well as, ' Tell me, good my lord,
What compass will you wear your farthingale ? '
Why even what fashion thou best lik'st, Lucetta.

Luc. You must needs have them with a codpiece, madam.

Jul. Out, out, Lucetta, that will be ill-favour'd.

Luc. A round hose, madam, now 's not worth a pin,
Unless you have a codpiece to stick pins on.

Jul. Lucetta, as thou lov'st me, let me have
What thou think'st meet, and is most mannerly.
But tell me, wench, how will the world repute me
For undertaking so unstaid a journey ?   60
I fear me it will make me scandaliz'd.

Luc. If you think so, then stay at home, and go not.

Jul. Nay, that I will not.

Luc. Then never dream on infamy, but go.
If Proteus like your journey, when you come,
No matter who 's displeas'd, when you are gone :
I fear me he will scarce be pleas'd withal.

Jul. That is the least, Lucetta, of my fear :
A thousand oaths, an ocean of his tears,
And instances of infinite of love,   70

Warrant me welcome to my Proteus.

Luc. All these are servants to deceitful men,

Jul. Base men, that use them to so base effect !
But truer stars did govern Proteus' birth :
His words are bonds, his oaths are oracles,
His love sincere, his thoughts immaculate,
His tears, pure messengers, sent from his heart,
His heart, as far from fraud as heaven from earth.

Luc. Pray heaven he prove so when you come to him !

Jul. Now, as thou lov'st me, do him not that wrong,   80
To bear a hard opinion of his truth :
Only deserve my love, by loving him,
And presently go with me to my chamber,
To take a note of what I stand in need of,
To furnish me upon my longing journey.
All that is mine I leave at thy dispose,
My goods, my lands, my reputation ;
Only, in lieu thereof, dispatch me hence.
Come ; answer not, but to it presently !
I am impatient of my tarriance.   *Exeunt* 90

Act Third

SCENE I

Milan.   Ante-room in the Duke's palace

Enter Duke, Thurio, and Proteus

Du. Sir Thurio, give us leave, I pray, awhile ;
　　We have some secrets to confer about.   *Exit Thurio*
　　Now, tell me, Proteus, what's your will with me ?
Pro. My gracious lord, that which I would discover
　　The law of friendship bids me to conceal,
　　But when I call to mind your gracious favours
　　Done to me, undeserving as I am,
　　My duty pricks me on to utter that
　　Which else no wordly good should draw from me.
　　Know, worthy prince, Sir Valentine, my friend,　　10
　　This night intends to steal away your daughter :
　　Myself am one made privy to the plot.
　　I know you have determin'd to bestow her
　　On Thurio, whom your gentle daughter hates,
　　And should she thus be stol'n away from you,
　　It would be much vexation to your age.
　　Thus, for my duty's sake, I rather chose

To cross my friend in his intended drift
Than, by concealing it, heap on your head
A pack of sorrows, which would press you down,   20
(Being unprevented) to your timeless grave.

Du. Proteus, I thank thee for thine honest care,
Which to requite, command me while I live.
This love of theirs myself have often seen,
Haply when they have judg'd me fast asleep,
And oftentimes have purpos'd to forbid
Sir Valentine her company and my court:
But, fearing lest my jealous aim might err,
And so (unworthily) disgrace the man,
(A rashness that I ever yet have shunn'd)   30
I gave him gentle looks, thereby to find
That which thyself hast now disclos'd to me.
And that thou may'st perceive my fear of this,
Knowing that tender youth is soon suggested,
I nightly lodge her in an upper tower,
The key whereof myself have ever kept;
And thence she cannot be convey'd away.

Pro. Know, noble lord, they have devis'd a mean
How he her chamber-window will ascend,
And with a corded ladder fetch her down;   40
For which the youthful lover now is gone,
And this way comes he with it presently;

Where, if it please you, you may intercept him.
But, good my Lord, do it so cunningly
That my discovery be not aimed at ;
For love of you, not hate unto my friend,
Hath made me publisher of this pretence.

Du. Upon mine honour, he shall never know
That I had any light from thee of this.

Pro. Adieu, my Lord, Sir Valentine is coming.   *Exit*   50

Enter Valentine

Du. Sir Valentine, whither away so fast ?

Val. Please it your grace, there is a messenger
That stays to bear my letters to my friends,
And I am going to deliver them.

Du. Be they of much import ?

Val. The tenour of them doth but signify
My health, and happy being at your court.

Du. Nay then, no matter ; stay with me awhile,
I am to break with thee of some affairs
That touch me near ; wherein thou must be secret.   60
'Tis not unknown to thee that I have sought
To match my friend Sir Thurio to my daughter.

Val. I know it well, my Lord, and, sure, the match
Were rich and honourable ; besides, the gentleman
Is full of virtue, bounty, worth, and qualities
Beseeming such a wife as your fair daughter :

Cannot your Grace win her to fancy him?

Du. No, trust me, she is peevish, sullen, froward,
    Proud, disobedient, stubborn, lacking duty,
    Neither regarding that she is my child,   70
    Nor fearing me, as if I were her father:
    And, may I say to thee, this pride of hers,
    Upon advice, hath drawn my love from her,
    And where I thought the remnant of mine age
    Should have been cherish'd by her child-like duty,
    I now am full resolv'd to take a wife,
    And turn her out to who will take her in:
    Then let her beauty be her wedding-dower;
    For me and my possessions she esteems not.

Val. What would your Grace have me to do in this?   80

Du. There is a lady in Verona here
    Whom I affect; but she is nice, and coy,
    And nought esteems my aged eloquence:
    Now, therefore, would I have thee to my tutor,
    (For long agone I have forgot to court,
    Besides, the fashion of the time is chang'd)
    How and which way I may bestow myself,
    To be regarded in her sun-bright eye.

Val. Win her with gifts, if she respect not words;
    Dumb jewels often in their silent kind   90
    More than quick words do move a woman's mind.

Du. But she did scorn a present that I sent her.

Val. A woman sometimes scorns what best contents her.
    Send her another ; never give her o'er ;
    For scorn at first makes after-love the more.
    If she do frown, 'tis not in hate of you,
    But rather to beget more love in you :
    If she do chide, 'tis not to have you gone ;
    For why, the fools are mad, if left alone.
    Take no repulse, whatever she doth say,   100
    For ' get you gone,' she doth not mean ' away ! '
    Flatter, and praise, commend, extol their graces ;
    Though ne'er so black, say they have angels' faces ;
    That man that hath a tongue, I say is no man,
    If with his tongue he cannot win a woman.

Du. But she I mean is promis'd by her friends
    Unto a youthful gentleman of worth,
    And kept severely from resort of men,
    That no man hath access by day to her.

Val. Why then I would resort to her by night.   110

Du. Ay, but the doors be lock'd, and keys kept safe,
    That no man hath recourse to her by night.

Val. What lets but one may enter at her window ?

Du. Her chamber is aloft, far from the ground,
    And built so shelving, that one cannot climb it
    Without apparent hazard of his life.

Val. Why then a ladder, quaintly made of cords,
　　To cast up, with a pair of anchoring hooks,
　　Would serve to scale another Hero's tower,
　　So bold Leander would adventure it.　　　　　　120
Du. Now, as thou art a gentleman of blood,
　　Advise me where I may have such a ladder.
Val. When would you use it? pray, sir, tell me that.
Du. This very night; for Love is like a child,
　　That longs for every thing that he can come by.
Val. By seven o'clock I'll get you such a ladder.
Du. But, hark thee; I will go to her alone:
　　How shall I best convey the ladder thither?
Val. It will be light, my lord, that you may bear it
　　Under a cloak that is of any length.　　　　　　130
Du. A cloak as long as thine will serve the turn?
Val. Ay, my good lord.
Du.　　　　　　　　Then let me see thy cloak:
　　I'll get me one of such another length.
Val. Why, any cloak will serve the turn, my lord.
Du. How shall I fashion me to wear a cloak?
　　I pray thee, let me feel thy cloak upon me.
　　What letter is this same? What's here? 'To
　　　　Silvia'!
　　And here an engine fit for my proceeding.
　　I'll be so bold to break the seal for once.　　　*Reads*

'My thoughts do harbour with my Silvia nightly,   140
   And slaves they are to me, that send them flying:
O, could their master come and go as lightly,
   Himself would lodge where senseless they are lying!
My herald thoughts in thy pure bosom rest them,
   While I, their king, that thither them importune,
Do curse the grace that with such grace hath bless'd
      them,
   Because myself do want my servants' fortune:
I curse myself, for they are sent by me,
That they should harbour where their lord should be.'
What's here?   150
   'Silvia, this night I will enfranchise thee.'
'Tis so; and here's the ladder for the purpose.
Why, Phaethon,—for thou art Merops' son,—   †
Wilt thou aspire to guide the heavenly car,
And with thy daring folly burn the world?
Wilt thou reach stars, because they shine on thee?
Go, base intruder, overweening slave,
Bestow thy fawning smiles on equal mates,
And think my patience, more than thy desert,
Is privilege for thy departure hence: 160
Thank me for this more than for all the favours,
Which, all too much, I have bestow'd on thee.
But if thou linger in my territories

Longer than swiftest expedition
Will give thee time to leave our royal court,
By heaven, my wrath shall far exceed the love
I ever bore my daughter, or thyself.
Be gone, I will not hear thy vain excuse,
But, as thou lov'st thy life, make speed from hence.

Exit

Val. And why not death, rather than living torment?   170
To die, is to be banish'd from myself,
And Silvia is myself : banish'd from her
Is self from self : ah deadly banishment !
What light is light, if Silvia be not seen ?
What joy is joy, if Silvia be not by ?
Unless it be to think that she is by,
And feed upon the shadow of perfection.
Except I be by Silvia in the night,
There is no music in the nightingale ;
Unless I look on Silvia in the day,   180
There is no day for me to look upon :
She is my essence, and I leave to be,
If I be not by her fair influence
Foster'd, illumin'd, cherish'd, kept alive.
I fly not death, to fly his deadly doom :
Tarry I here, I but attend on death,
But fly I hence, I fly away from life.

Enter Proteus and Launce

Pro. Run, boy, run, run, and seek him out.

Lau. Soho, soho !

Pro. What seest thou ?   190

Lau. Him we go to find : there 's not a hair on 's head but
  'tis a Valentine.

Pro. Valentine ?

Val. No.

Pro. Who then ? his spirit ?

Val. Neither.

Pro. What then ?

Val. Nothing.

Lau. Can nothing speak ?   Master, shall I strike ?

Pro. Who wouldst thou strike ?   200

Lau. Nothing.

Pro. Villain, forbear.

Lau. Why, sir, I 'll strike nothing : I pray you,—

Pro. Sirrah, I say forbear.   Friend Valentine, a word.

Val. My ears are stopt, and cannot hear good news,
  So much of bad already hath possess'd them.

Pro. Then in dumb silence will I bury mine,
  For they are harsh, untuneable, and bad.

Val. Is Silvia dead ?

Pro. No, Valentine.   210

Val. No Valentine, indeed, for sacred Silvia.

Hath she forsworn me?

Pro. No, Valentine.

Val. No Valentine, if Silvia have forsworn me.
　　What is your news?

Lau. Sir, there is a proclamation that you are vanished.　　†

Pro. That thou art banished—O, that's the news!—
　　From hence, from Silvia, and from me thy friend.

Val. O, I have fed upon this woe already,
　　And now excess of it will make me surfeit.　　220
　　Doth Silvia know that I am banished?

Pro. Ay, ay; and she hath offer'd to the doom
　　(Which unrevers'd stands in effectual force)
　　A sea of melting pearl, which some call tears;
　　Those at her father's churlish feet she tender'd,
　　With them, upon her knees, her humble self,
　　Wringing her hands, whose whiteness so became them
　　As if but now they waxed pale for woe:
　　But neither bended knees, pure hands held up,
　　Sad sighs, deep groans, nor silver-shedding tears,　　230
　　Could penetrate her uncompassionate sire;
　　But Valentine, if he be ta'en, must die.
　　Besides, her intercession chaf'd him so,
　　When she for thy repeal was suppliant,
　　That to close prison he commanded her,
　　With many bitter threats of biding there.

Val. No more ; unless the next word that thou speak'st
　　　Have some malignant power upon my life :
　　　If so, I pray thee breathe it in mine ear,
　　　As ending anthem of my endless dolour.　　　　　240
Pro. Cease to lament for that thou canst not help,
　　　And study help for that which thou lament'st.
　　　Time is the nurse and breeder of all good ;
　　　Here, if thou stay, thou canst not see thy love ;
　　　Besides, thy staying will abridge thy life :
　　　Hope is a lover's staff, walk hence with that,
　　　And manage it against despairing thoughts :
　　　Thy letters may be here, though thou art hence,
　　　Which, being writ to me, shall be deliver'd
　　　Even in the milk-white bosom of thy love.　　　　250
　　　The time now serves not to expostulate,
　　　Come, I 'll convey thee through the city-gate ;
　　　And ere I part with thee, confer at large
　　　Of all that may concern thy love-affairs.
　　　As thou lov'st Silvia (though not for thyself)
　　　Regard thy danger, and along with me !
Val. I pray thee, Launce, an if thou seest my boy,
　　　Bid him make haste, and meet me at the Northgate.
Pro. Go, sirrah, find him out.　Come, Valentine.
Val. O my dear Silvia !　Hapless Valentine !　　　　260

　　　　　　　　　　Exeunt Valentine and Proteus

Lau. I am but a fool, look you ; and yet I have the wit
to think my master is a kind of a knave : but that's
all one, if he be but one knave.   He lives not now
that knows me to be in love, yet I am in love, but
a team of horse shall not pluck that from me ; nor
who 'tis I love ; and yet 'tis a woman ; but what
woman, I will not tell myself ; and yet 'tis a milk-
maid ; yet 'tis not a maid ; for she hath had gossips ;
yet 'tis a maid, for she is her master's maid, and
serves for wages.   She hath more qualities than a   270
water-spaniel,—which is much in a bare Christian.
(*Pulling out a paper.*)   Here is the catalogue of her
condition.   ' Imprimis : She can fetch and carry.'
Why, a horse can do no more : nay, a horse cannot
fetch, but only carry, therefore is she better than a
jade.   ' Item : She can milk ' ; look you, a sweet
virtue in a maid with clean hands.

Enter Speed

Sp. How now, Signior Launce ?   what news with your
mastership ?

Lau. With my master's ship ?   why, it is at sea.   280

Sp. Well, your old vice still ; mistake the word.   What
news then in your paper ?

Lau. The black'st news that ever thou heard'st.

Sp. Why, man ? how black ?

Lau. Why, as black as ink.

Sp. Let me read them.

Lau. Fie on thee, jolt-head, thou canst not read.

Sp. Thou liest ; I can.

Lau. I will try thee.   Tell me this : who begot thee ?

Sp. Marry, the son of my grandfather.   290

Lau. O illiterate loiterer ! it was the son of thy grand-
mother : this proves that thou canst not read.

Sp. Come, fool, come ; try me in thy paper.

Lau. There ; and Saint Nicholas be thy speed !

Sp. (*reads*) 'Imprimis : She can milk.'

Lau. Ay, that she can.

Sp. 'Item : She brews good ale.'

Lau. And thereof comes the proverb : 'Blessing of your
heart, you brew good ale.'

Sp. 'Item : She can sew.'   300

Lau. That 's as much as to say, 'Can she so ? '

Sp. 'Item : She can knit.'

Lau. What need a man care for a stock with a wench,
when she can knit him a stock ?

Sp. 'Item : She can wash and scour.'

Lau. A special virtue ; for then she need not be wash'd
and scour'd.

Sp. 'Item : She can spin.'

Lau. Then may I set the world on wheels, when she can
spin for her living.   310

Sp. ' Item : She hath many nameless vitrues.'

Lau. That's as much as to say, bastard virtues ; that
indeed know not their fathers ; and therefore have
no names.

Sp. Here follow her vices.

Lau. Close at the heels of her virtues.

Sp. ' Item : She is not to be kissed fasting, in respect of
her breath.'

Lau. Well, that fault may be mended with a breakfast.
Read on.   320

Sp. ' Item : She hath a sweet mouth.'

Lau. That makes amends for her sour breath.

Sp. ' Item : She doth talk in her sleep.'

Lau. It's no matter for that ; so she sleep not in her talk.

Sp. ' Item : She is slow in words.'

Lau. O villain, that set this down among her vices !   To
be slow in words is a woman's only virtue : I pray
thee, out with 't, and place it for her chief virtue.

Sp. ' Item : She is proud.'

Lau. Out with that too ; it was Eve's legacy, and cannot   330
be ta'en from her.

Sp. ' Item : She hath no teeth.'

Lau. I care not for that neither ; because I love crusts.

Sp. ' Item : She is curst.'

Lau. Well, the best is, she hath no teeth to bite.

Sp. ' Item : She will often praise her liquor.'

Lau. If her liquor be good, she shall : if she will not, I will ; for good things should be praised.

Sp. ' Item : She is too liberal.'

Lau. Of her tongue she cannot ; for that 's writ down she 340 is slow of ; of her purse, she shall not, for that I 'll keep shut : now, of another thing she may, and that cannot I help.   Well, proceed.

Sp. ' Item : She hath more hair than wit, and more faults than hairs, and more wealth than faults.'

Lau. Stop there ; I 'll have her : she was mine and not mine, twice or thrice in that last article.   Rehearse that once more.

Sp. ' Item : She hath more hair than wit,'—

Lau. More hair than wit ?   It may be I 'll prove it.   The 350 cover of the salt hides the salt, and therefore it is more than the salt ; the hair that covers the wit is more than the wit, for the greater hides the less. What 's next ?

Sp. ' And more faults than hairs,'—

Lau. That 's monstrous :   O, that that were out !

Sp. ' And more wealth than faults.'

Lau. Why, that word makes the faults gracious.   Well,

I 'll have her : and if it be a match, as nothing is
impossible,—   360

Sp. What then ?

Lau. Why, then will I tell thee—that thy master stays for
thee at the North-gate ?

Sp. For me ?

Lau. For thee ! ay, who art thou ? he hath stay'd for a
better man than thee.

Sp. And must I go to him ?

Lau. Thou must run to him ; for thou hast stay'd so long,
that going will scarce serve the turn.

Sp. Why didst not tell me sooner ? pox of your love- 370
letters !   *Exit*

Lau. Now will he be swing'd for reading my letter—an
unmannerly slave, that will thrust himself into
secrets ! I 'll after, to rejoice in the boy's correction.
                                             Exit

SCENE II

The same.   The Duke's palace

Enter Duke and Thurio

Du. Sir Thurio, fear not but that she will love you,
    Now Valentine is banish'd from her sight.

Thu. Since his exile she hath despis'd me most,

Forsworn my company, and rail'd at me,
That I am desperate of obtaining her.

Du. This weak impress of love is as a figure
Trenched in ice, which with an hour's heat
Dissolves to water, and doth lose his form.
A little time will melt her frozen thoughts,
And worthless Valentine shall be forgot.　　　　10

Enter Proteus

How now, Sir Proteus ?　Is your countryman,
According to our proclamation, gone ?

Pro. Gone, my good lord.

Du. My daughter takes his going grievously.

Pro. A little time, my lord, will kill that grief.

Du. So I believe ; but Thurio thinks not so.
Proteus, the good conceit I hold of thee
(For thou hast shown some sign of good desert)
Makes me the better to confer with thee.

Pro. Longer than I prove loyal to your Grace　　　20
Let me not live, to look upon your Grace.

Du. Thou know'st how willingly I would effect
The match between Sir Thurio and my daughter ?

Pro. I do, my lord.

Du. And also, I think, thou art not ignorant
How she opposes her against my will ?

Pro. She did, my lord, when Valentine was here.

Du. Ay, and perversely she persevers so.
    What might we do to make the girl forget
    The love of Valentine, and love Sir Thurio?   30

Pro. The best way is, to slander Valentine,
    With falsehood, cowardice, and poor descent,
    Three things that women highly hold in hate.

Du. Ay, but she 'll think that it is spoke in hate.

Pro. Ay, if his enemy deliver it :
    Therefore it must with circumstance be spoken
    By one whom she esteemeth as his friend.

Du. Then you must undertake to slander him.

Pro. And that, my lord, I shall be loath to do :
    'Tis an ill office for a gentleman,   40
    Especially against his very friend.

Du. Where your good word cannot advantage him,
    Your slander never can endamage him ;
    Therefore the office is indifferent,
    Being entreated to it by your friend.

Pro. You have prevail'd, my lord : if I can do it
    By aught that I can speak in his dispraise,
    She shall not long continue love to him.
    But say this weed her love from Valentine,
    It follows not that she will love Sir Thurio.   50

Thu. Therefore, as you unwind her love from him,
    Lest it should ravel, and be good to none,

      You must provide to bottom it on me ;
      Which must be done by praising me as much
      As you in worth dispraise Sir Valentine.

Du. And, Proteus, we dare trust you in this kind,
      Because we know, on Valentine's report,
      You are already Love's firm votary,
      And cannot soon revolt, and change your mind.
      Upon this warrant shall you have access   60
      Where you with Silvia may confer at large ;
      For she is lumpish, heavy, melancholy,
      And, for your friend's sake, will be glad of you ;
      Where you may temper her, by your persuasion,
      To hate young Valentine, and love my friend.

Pro. As much as I can do, I will effect :
      But you, Sir Thurio, are not sharp enough ;
      You must lay lime, to tangle her desires
      By wailful sonnets, whose composed rhymes
      Should be full-fraught with serviceable vows.   70

Du. Ay,
      Much is the force of heaven-bred poesy.

Pro. Say that upon the altar of her beauty
      You sacrifice your tears, your sighs, your heart :
      Write till your ink be dry, and with your tears
      Moist it again ; and frame some feeling line
      That may discover such integrity :   †

For Orpheus' lute was strung with poets' sinews,
Whose golden touch could soften steel and stones,
Make tigers tame, and huge leviathans   80
Forsake unsounded deeps, to dance on sands.
After your dire-lamenting elegies,
Visit by night your lady's chamber-window
With some sweet consort ; to their instruments
Tune a deploring dump : the night's dead silence
Will well become such sweet complaining grievance.
This, or else nothing, will inherit her.

Du. This discipline shows thou hast been in love.

Thu. And thy advice this night I 'll put in practice.
Therefore, sweet Proteus, my direction-giver,   90
Let us into the city presently
To sort some gentlemen, well skill'd in music.
I have a sonnet that will serve the turn
To give the onset to thy good advice.

Du. About it, gentlemen !

Pro. We 'll wait upon your Grace till after supper,
And afterward determine our proceedings.

Du. Even now about it !   I will pardon you.   *Exeunt*

Act Fourth

SCENE I

The frontiers of Mantua.   A forest

Enter certain Outlaws

1.*O.* Fellows, stand fast ; I see a passenger.

2.*O.* If there be ten, shrink not, but down with 'em.

Enter Valentine and Speed

3.*O.* Stand, sir, and throw us that you have about ye :
    If not, we 'll make you sit, and rifle you.

Sp. Sir, we are undone ; these are the villains
    That all the travellers do fear so much.

Val. My friends,—

1.*O.* That 's not so, sir : we are your enemies.

2.*O.* Peace ! we 'll hear him.

3.*O.* Ay, by my beard, will we ; for he 's a proper man.   10

Val. Then know that I have little wealth to lose :
    A man I am cross'd with adversity ;
    My riches are these poor habiliments,
    Of which if you should here disfurnish me,
    You take the sum and substance that I have.

2.*O.* Whither travel you ?

Val. To Verona.

1.*O.* Whence came you ?

Val. From Milan.

3.*O.* Have you long sojourn'd there ?   20

Val. Some sixteen months, and longer might have stay'd,
        If crooked fortune had not thwarted me.

1.*O.* What, were you banish'd thence ?

Val. I was.

2.*O.* For what offence ?

Val. For that which now torments me to rehearse :
        I kill'd a man, whose death I much repent,   †
        But yet I slew him manfully, in fight,
        Without false vantage, or base treachery.

1.*O.* Why, ne'er repent it, if it were done so ;   30
        But were you banish'd for so small a fault ?

Val. I was, and held me glad of such a doom.

2.*O.* Have you the tongues ?

Val. My youthful travel therein made me happy,
        Or else I often had been miserable.

3.*O.* By the bare scalp of Robin Hood's fat friar,
        This fellow were a king for our wild faction !

1.*O.* We 'll have him.   Sirs, a word.

Sp. Master, be one of them ; it 's an honourable kind
        of thievery.   40

Val. Peace, villain !

2.*O.* Tell us this : have you any thing to take to ?
Val. Nothing but my fortune.
3.*O.* Know then, that some of us are gentlemen,
  Such as the fury of ungovern'd youth
  Thrust from the company of awful men :
  Myself was from Verona banished
  For practising to steal away a lady,
  An heir, and near allied unto the duke.
2.*O.* And I from Mantua, for a gentleman,   50
  Who, in my mood, I stabb'd unto the heart.
1.*O.* And I for such like petty crimes as these.
  But to the purpose,—for we cite our faults,
  That they may hold excus'd our lawless lives ;
  And partly, seeing you are beautified
  With goodly shape ; and by your own report
  A linguist, and a man of such perfection
  As we do in our quality much want,—
2.*O.* Indeed, because you are a banish'd man,
  Therefore, above the rest, we parley to you : 60
  Are you content to be our general ?
  To make a virtue of necessity,
  And live, as we do, in this wilderness ?
3.*O.* What say'st thou ? wilt thou be of our consort ?
  Say ay, and be the captain of us all :
  We 'll do thee homage, and be rul'd by thee,

Love thee, as our commander, and our king.

1.O. But if thou scorn our courtesy, thou diest.

2.O. Thou shalt not live, to brag what we have offer'd.

Val. I take your offer, and will live with you,   70
  Provided that you do no outrages
  On silly women, or poor passengers.

3.O. No, we detest such vile base practices.
  Come, go with us, we'll bring thee to our crews,
  And show thee all the treasure we have got;
  Which, with ourselves, all rest at thy dispose.

           Exeunt

SCENE II

*Milan. Outside the Duke's palace,
under Silvia's chamber*

Enter Proteus

Pro. Already have I been false to Valentine,
  And now I must be as unjust to Thurio;
  Under the colour of commending him,
  I have access my own love to prefer:
  But Silvia is too fair, too true, too holy,
  To be corrupted with my worthless gifts;
  When I protest true loyalty to her,

She twits me with my falsehood to my friend ;
When to her beauty I commend my vows,
She bids me think how I have been forsworn 10
In breaking faith with Julia, whom I lov'd :
And notwithstanding all her sudden quips,
The least whereof would quell a lover's hope,
Yet, spaniel-like, the more she spurns my love,
The more it grows, and fawneth on her still.
But here comes Thurio : now must we to her window
And give some evening music to her ear.

Enter Thurio and Musicians

Thu. Here now, Sir Proteus, are you crept before us ?
Pro. Ay, gentle Thurio ; for you know that love
Will creep in service where it cannot go. 20
Thu. Ay, but I hope, sir, that you love not here.
Pro. Sir, but I do ; or else I would be hence.
Thu. Who ? Silvia ?
Pro.   Ay, Silvia, for your sake.
Thu. I thank you for your own.   Now, gentlemen,
Let 's tune, and to it lustily awhile.

Enter, at a distance, Host, and Julia in boy's clothes

Ho. Now, my young guest, methinks you 're allycholly :
I pray you, why is it ?
Jul. Marry, mine host, because I cannot be merry.
Ho. Come, we 'll have you merry ; I 'll bring you where

you shall hear music, and see the gentleman that   30
you ask'd for.

Jul. But shall I hear him speak ?

Ho. Ay, that you shall.

Jul. That will be music.   *Music plays*

Ho. Hark, hark !

Jul. Is he among these ?

Ho. Ay : but, peace ! let 's hear 'em.

SONG

Who is Silvia ? what is she ?
   That all our swains commend her ?
Holy, fair, and wise is she ;   40
   The heaven such grace did lend her,
That she might admired be.

Is she kind as she is fair ?
   For beauty lives with kindness :
Love doth to her eyes repair,
   To help him of his blindness,
And, being help'd, inhabits there.

Then to Silvia let us sing,
   That Silvia is excelling ;
She excels each mortal thing   50
   Upon the dull earth dwelling :
To her let us garlands bring.

71

Ho. How now? are you sadder than you were before?
How do you, man? the music likes you not.

Jul. You mistake; the musician likes me not.

Ho. Why, my pretty youth?

Jul. He plays false, father.

Ho. How? out of tune on the strings?

Jul. Not so; but yet so false that he grieves my very
heart-strings.   60

Ho. You have a quick ear.

Jul. Ay, I would I were deaf; it makes me have a slow
heart.

Ho. I perceive you delight not in music.

Jul. Not a whit, when it jars so.

Ho. Hark, what fine change is in the music!

Jul. Ay; that change is the spite.

Ho. You would have them always play but one thing?

Jul. I would always have one play but one thing.
But, host, doth this Sir Proteus that we talk on   70
Often resort unto this gentlewoman?

Ho. I tell you what Launce, his man, told me,—he lov'd
her out of all nick.

Jul. Where is Launce?

Ho. Gone to seek his dog, which to-morrow, by his
master's command, he must carry for a present to
his lady.

72

Jul. Peace ! stand aside : the company parts.

Pro. Sir Thurio, fear not you ; I will so plead,
That you shall say my cunning drift excels.   80

Thu. Where meet we ?

Pro.   At Saint Gregory's well.

Thu.   Farewell.

Exeunt Thurio and Musicians
Enter Silvia above

Pro. Madam, good even to your ladyship.

Sil. I thank you for your music, gentlemen.
Who is that that spake ?

Pro. One, lady, if you knew his pure heart's truth,
You would quickly learn to know him by his voice.

Sil. Sir Proteus, as I take it.

Pro. Sir Proteus, gentle lady, and your servant.

Sil. What 's your will ?

Pro.   That I may compass yours.

Sil. You have your wish ; my will is even this,   90
That presently you hie you home to bed.
Thou subtle, perjur'd, false, disloyal man !
Think'st thou I am so shallow, so conceitless,
To be seduced by thy flattery,
That hast deceiv'd so many with thy vows ?
Return, return, and make thy love amends :
For me (by this pale queen of night I swear)

73

  I am so far from granting thy request,
  That I despise thee, for thy wrongful suit;
  And by and by intend to chide myself   100
  Even for this time I spend in talking to thee.
Pro. I grant, sweet love, that I did love a lady,
  But she is dead.
Jul. (*aside*) 'Twere false, if I should speak it;
  For I am sure she is not buried.
Sil. Say that she be; yet Valentine thy friend
  Survives; to whom (thyself art witness)
  I am betroth'd; and art thou not asham'd
  To wrong him with thy importunacy?
Pro. I likewise hear that Valentine is dead.   110
Sil. And so suppose am I; for in his grave
  Assure thyself my love is buried.
Pro. Sweet lady, let me rake it from the earth.
Sil. Go to thy lady's grave and call hers thence,
  Or, at the least, in hers sepulchre thine.
Jul. (*aside*) He heard not that.
Pro. Madam, if your heart be so obdurate,
  Vouchsafe me yet your picture for my love,
  The picture that is hanging in your chamber;
  To that I 'll speak, to that I 'll sigh and weep: 120
  For since the substance of your perfect self
  Is else devoted, I am but a shadow;

And to your shadow will I make true love.

Jul. (*aside*) If 'twere a substance, you would sure deceive it,
And make it but a shadow, as I am.

Sil. I am very loath to be your idol, sir ;
But, since your falsehood shall become you well
To worship shadows, and adore false shapes,
Send to me in the morning, and I 'll send it :
And so, good rest.

Pro.   As wretches have o'ernight   130
That wait for execution in the morn.

Exeunt Proteus and Silvia severally

Jul. Host, will you go ?

Ho. By my halidom, I was fast asleep.

Jul. Pray you, where lies Sir Proteus ?

Ho. Marry, at my house.   Trust me, I think 'tis almost
day.

Jul. Not so ; but it hath been the longest night
That e'er I watch'd, and the most heaviest.   *Exeunt*

SCENE III

The same

Enter Eglamour

Egl. This is the hour that Madam Silvia
Entreated me to call and know her mind :

There's some great matter she'ld employ me in.
Madam, madam !

Enter Silvia above

Sil. Who calls ?
Egl. Your servant and your friend ;
One that attends your ladyship's command.
Sil. Sir Eglamour, a thousand times good morrow.
Egl. As many, worthy lady, to yourself :
According to your ladyship's impose,
I am thus early come, to know what service
It is your pleasure to command me in. 10
Sil. O Eglamour, thou art a gentleman,—
Think not I flatter, for I swear I do not,—
Valiant, wise, remorseful, well accomplish'd :
Thou art not ignorant what dear good will
I bear unto the banish'd Valentine ;
Nor how my father would enforce me marry
Vain Thurio, whom my very soul abhors.
Thyself hast lov'd, and I have heard thee say
No grief did ever come so near thy heart
As when thy lady and thy true love died, 20
Upon whose grave thou vow'dst pure chastity.
Sir Eglamour, I would to Valentine,
To Mantua, where I hear he makes abode ;
And, for the ways are dangerous to pass,

I do desire thy worthy company,
Upon whose faith and honour I repose.
Urge not my father's anger, Eglamour,
But think upon my grief, a lady's grief,
And on the justice of my flying hence,
To keep me from a most unholy match,   30
Which heaven and fortune still rewards with plagues.
I do desire thee, even from a heart
As full of sorrows as the sea of sands,
To bear me company, and go with me :
If not, to hide what I have said to thee,
That I may venture to depart alone.

Egl. Madam, I pity much your grievances ;
Which since I know they virtuously are plac'd,
I give consent to go along with you,
Recking as little what betideth me,   40
As much I wish all good befortune you.
When will you go ?

Sil.   This evening coming.

Egl. Where shall I meet you ?

Sil.   At Friar Patrick's cell,
Where I intend holy confession.

Egl. I will not fail your ladyship.   Good morrow, gentle
lady.

Sil.   Good morrow, kind Sir Eglamour.   *Exeunt severally*

SCENE IV

The same

Enter Launce, with his Dog

Lau. When a man's servant shall play the cur with him, look you, it goes hard : one that I brought up of a puppy ; one that I sav'd from drowning, when three or four of his blind brothers and sisters went to it ! I have taught him, even as one would say precisely, ' thus I would teach a dog.' I was sent to deliver him as a present to Mistress Silvia from my master ; and I came no sooner into the dining-chamber, but he steps me to her trencher, and steals her capon's leg : O, 'tis a foul thing when a cur 10 cannot keep himself in all companies ! I would have, as one should say, one that takes upon him to be a dog indeed, to be, as it were, a dog at all things. If I had not had more wit than he, to take a fault upon me that he did, I think verily he had been hang'd for 't ; sure as I live, he had suffer'd for 't : you shall judge. He thrusts me himself into the company of three or four gentlemanlike dogs, under the duke's table : he had not been there (bless the mark) a pissing while, but all the chamber smelt 20

him. 'Out with the dog!' says one: 'What cur
is that?' says another: 'Whip him out,' says the
third: 'Hang him up,' says the duke. I, having
been acquainted with the smell before, knew it was
Crab, and goes me to the fellow that whips the
dogs: 'Friend,' quoth I, 'you mean to whip the
dog?' 'Ay, marry, do I,' quoth he. 'You do
him the more wrong,' quoth I; ''twas I did the
thing you wot of.' He makes me no more ado, but
whips me out of the chamber. How many masters   30
would do this for his servant? Nay, I 'll be sworn,
I have sat in the stocks for puddings he hath stolen,
otherwise he had been executed; I have stood on
the pillory for geese he hath kill'd, otherwise he had
suffer'd for 't. Thou think'st not of this now.
Nay, I remember the trick you serv'd me when I
took my leave of Madam Silvia: did not I bid thee †
still mark me, and do as I do? when didst thou see
me heave up my leg, and make water against a
gentlewoman's farthingale? didst thou ever see me   40
do such a trick?

Enter Proteus and Julia

Pro. Sebastian is thy name? I like thee well,
And will employ thee in some service presently.
Jul. In what you please, I 'll do what I can.

Pro. I hope thou wilt. (*to Launce*) How now, you
    whoreson peasant,
    Where have you been these two days loitering ?

Lau. Marry, sir, I carried Mistress Silvia the dog you bade
    me.

Pro. And what says she to my little jewel ?

Lau. Marry, she says your dog was a cur, and tells you   50
    currish thanks is good enough for such a present.

Pro. But she receiv'd my dog ?

Lau. No, indeed, did she not : here have I brought him
    back again.

Pro. What, didst thou offer her this from me ?

Lau. Ay, sir ; the other squirrel was stolen from me by
    the hangman's boys in the market-place : and then
    I offer'd her mine own, who is a dog as big as ten
    of yours, and therefore the gift the greater.

Pro. Go get thee hence, and find my dog again,   60
    Or ne'er return again into my sight.
    Away, I say ! stay'st thou to vex me here ?

                      Exit Launce

    A slave, that still an end turns me to shame !
    Sebastian, I have entertained thee,
    Partly that I have need of such a youth,
    That can with some discretion do my business,
    For 'tis no trusting to yond foolish lout ;

But chiefly for thy face and thy behaviour,
Which (if my augury deceive me not)
Witness good bringing up, fortune, and truth :   70
Therefore know thou, for this I entertain thee.
Go presently, and take this ring with thee,
Deliver it to Madam Silvia :
She lov'd me well deliver'd it to me.

Jul. It seems you lov'd not her, to leave her token.
She is dead, belike ?

Pro.   Not so ; I think she lives.

Jul. Alas !

Pro. Why dost thou cry, ' alas ' ?

Jul.   I cannot choose
But pity her.

Pro.   Wherefore shouldst thou pity her ?

Jul. Because methinks that she lov'd you as well   80
As you do love your lady Silvia :
She dreams on him that has forgot her love ;
You dote on her that cares not for your love.
'Tis pity, love should be so contrary ;
And thinking on it makes me cry, ' alas ! '

Pro. Well, give her that ring, and therewithal
This letter ; that 's her chamber : tell my lady
I claim the promise for her heavenly picture
Your message done, hie home unto my chamber,

Where thou shalt find me sad and solitary.   *Exit* 90

Jul. How many women would do such a message?
Alas, poor Proteus! thou hast entertain'd
A fox, to be the shepherd of thy lambs.
Alas, poor fool, why do I pity him
That with his very heart despiseth me?
Because he loves her, he despiseth me,
Because I love him, I must pity him.
This ring I gave him, when he parted from me,
To bind him to remember my good will;
And now am I (unhappy messenger)   100
To plead for that which I would not obtain,
To carry that which I would have refus'd,
To praise his faith which I would have disprais'd.
I am my master's true-confirmed love,
But cannot be true servant to my master,
Unless I prove false traitor to myself.
Yet will I woo for him, but yet so coldly,
As (heaven it knows) I would not have him speed.

Enter Silvia, attended

Gentlewoman, good day! I pray you, be my mean
To bring me where to speak with Madam Silvia.   110

Sil. What would you with her, if that I be she?

Jul. If you be she, I do entreat your patience
To hear me speak the message I am sent on.

Sil. From whom ?

Jul. From my master, Sir Proteus, madam.

Sil. O, he sends you for a picture.

Jul. Ay, madam.

Sil. Ursula, bring my picture there ;
    Go give your master this : tell him, from me,
    One Julia, that his changing thoughts forget,   120
    Would better fit his chamber than this shadow.

Jul. Madam, please you peruse this letter.—
    Pardon me, madam ; I have unadvis'd
    Deliver'd you a paper that I should not :
    This is the letter to your ladyship.

Sil. I pray thee, let me look on that again.

Jul. It may not be ; good madam, pardon me.

Sil. There, hold !
    I will not look upon your master's lines :
    I know they are stuff'd with protestations,   130
    And full of new-found oaths, which he will break
    As easily as I do tear his paper.

Jul. Madam, he sends your ladyship this ring.

Sil. The more shame for him that he sends it me ;
    For I have heard him say a thousand times
    His Julia gave it him, at his departure :
    Though his false finger have profan'd the ring,
    Mine shall not do his Julia so much wrong.

Jul. She thanks you.

Sil. What say'st thou ?   140

Jul. I thank you, madam, that you tender her :
　　Poor gentlewoman ! my master wrongs her much.

Sil. Dost thou know her ?

Jul. Almost as well as I do know myself :
　　To think upon her woes, I do protest
　　That I have wept a hundred several times.

Sil. Belike she thinks that Proteus hath forsook her.

Jul. I think she doth ; and that 's her cause of sorrow.

Sil. Is she not passing fair ?

Jul. She hath been fairer, madam, than she is :   150
　　When she did think my master lov'd her well,
　　She, in my judgement, was as fair as you ;
　　But since she did neglect her looking-glass,
　　And threw her sun-expelling mask away,
　　The air hath starv'd the roses in her cheeks,
　　And pinch'd the lily-tincture of her face,
　　That now she is become as black as I.

Sil. How tall was she ?

Jul. About my stature : for, at Pentecost,
　　When all our pageants of delight were play'd,   160
　　Our youth got me to play the woman's part,
　　And I was trimm'd in Madam Julia's gown ;
　　Which served me as fit, by all men's judgements,

As if the garment had been made for me :
Therefore I know she is about my height.
And at that time I made her weep agood,
For I did play a lamentable part :
Madam, 'twas Ariadne passioning
For Theseus' perjury and unjust flight ;
Which I so lively acted with my tears,   170
That my poor mistress, moved therewithal,
Wept bitterly ; and, would I might be dead,
If I in thought felt not her very sorrow !

Sil. She is beholding to thee, gentle youth ;
Alas, poor lady, desolate and left !
I weep myself to think upon thy words.
Here, youth ; there is my purse ; I give thee this
For thy sweet mistress' sake, because thou lov'st her.
Farewell.   *Exit Silvia, with attendants*

Jul. And she shall thank you for' t, if e'er you know her.   180
A virtuous gentlewoman, mild and beautiful !
I hope my master's suit will be but cold,
Since she respects my mistress' love so much.
Alas, how love can trifle with itself !
Here is her picture : let me see ; I think,
If I had such a tire, this face of mine
Were full as lovely as is this of hers :
And yet the painter flatter'd her a little,

Unless I flatter with myself too much.
Her hair is auburn, mine is perfect yellow ;   190
If that be all the difference in his love,
I 'll get me such a colour'd periwig.
Her eyes are grey as glass ; and so are mine :
Ay, but her forehead 's low, and mine 's as high :
What should it be that he respects in her,
But I can make respective in myself,
If this fond Love were not a blinded god ?
Come, shadow, come, and take this shadow up,
For 'tis thy rival : O thou senseless form,
Thou shalt be worshipp'd, kiss'd, lov'd, and ador'd ! 200
And, were there sense in his idolatry,
My substance should be statue in thy stead.
I 'll use thee kindly, for thy mistress' sake,
That us'd me so ; or else, by Jove I vow,
I should have scratch'd out your unseeing eyes,
To make my master out of love with thee !   *Exit*

Act Fifth

SCENE I

Milan.   An abbey

Enter Eglamour

Egl. The sun begins to gild the western sky,
And now it is about the very hour
That Silvia, at Friar Patrick's cell, should meet me.
She will not fail ; for lovers break not hours,
Unless it be to come before their time,
So much they spur their expedition.
See where she comes.

Enter Silvia

Lady, a happy evening !

Sil. Amen, amen !   Go on, good Eglamour,
Out at the postern by the abbey-wall :
I fear I am attended by some spies.   10

Egl. Fear not : the forest is not three leagues off,
If we recover that, we are sure enough.   *Exeunt*

SCENE II

The same.   The Duke's palace

Enter Thurio, Proteus, and Julia

Thu. Sir Proteus, what says Silvia to my suit ?

Pro. O, sir, I find her milder than she was ;
   And yet she takes exceptions at your person.

Thu. What ? that my leg is too long ?

Pro. No, that it is too little.

Thu. I 'll wear a boot, to make it somewhat rounder.

Jul. (*aside*) But love will not be spurr'd to what it loathes.

Thu. What says she to my face ?

Pro. She says it is a fair one.

Thu. Nay then, the wanton lies ; my face is black.   10

Pro. But pearls are fair ; and the old saying is,
   Black men are pearls, in beauteous ladies' eyes.

Jul. (*aside*) 'Tis true, such pearls as put out ladies' eyes,
   For I had rather wink than look on them.

Thu. How likes she my discourse ?

Pro. Ill, when you talk of war.

Thu. But well, when I discourse of love and peace.

Jul. (*aside*) But better indeed when you hold your peace.

Thu. What says she to my valour ?

Pro. O sir, she makes no doubt of that.   20

Jul. (*aside*) She needs not, when she knows it cowardice.

Thu. What says she to my birth ?

Pro. That you are well deriv'd.

Jul. (*aside*) True ; from a gentleman, to a fool.

Thu. Considers she my possessions ?

Pro. O, ay ; and pities them.

Thu. Wherefore ?

Jul. (*aside*) That such an ass should owe them.

Pro. That they are out by lease.

Jul. Here comes the duke.   30

Enter Duke

Du. How now, Sir Proteus ; how now, Thurio ?
　　　Which of you saw Sir Eglamour of late ?

Thu. Not I.

Pro.　　　Nor I.

Du.　　　　　　　Saw you my daughter ?

Pro.　　　　　　　　　　　Neither.

Du. Why then,
　　　She 's fled unto that peasant Valentine ;
　　　And Eglamour is in her company.
　　　'Tis true ; for Friar Laurence met them both,
　　　As he in penance wander'd through the forest ;
　　　Him he knew well ; and guess'd that it was she,
　　　But, being mask'd, he was not sure of it ;   40
　　　Besides, she did intend confession

89

At Patrick's cell this even, and there she was not ;
These likelihoods confirm her flight from hence ;
Therefore I pray you, stand not to discourse,
But mount you presently, and meet with me
Upon the rising of the mountain-foot
That leads toward Mantua, whither they are fled :
Dispatch, sweet gentlemen, and follow me.   *Exit*

Thu. Why this it is, to be a peevish girl,
That flies her fortune when it follows her :   50
I 'll after ; more to be reveng'd on Eglamour
Than for the love of reckless Silvia.   *Exit*

Pro. And I will follow, more for Silvia's love
Than hate of Eglamour that goes with her.   *Exit*

Jul. And I will follow, more to cross that love
Than hate for Silvia, that is gone for love.   *Exit*

SCENE III

The frontiers of Mantua.   The forest

Enter Outlaws with Silvia

1.*O.* Come, come,
Be patient ; we must bring you to our captain.

Sil. A thousand more mischances than this one
Have learn'd me how to brook this patiently.

2.*O.* Come, bring her away.

1.*O.* Where is the gentleman that was with her ?

3.*O.* Being nimble-footed, he hath outrun us,
    But Moses and Valerius follow him.
    Go thou with her to the west end of the wood,
    There is our captain : we 'll follow him that 's fled,   10
    The thicket is beset, he cannot 'scape.

1.*O.* Come, I must bring you to our captain's cave :
    Fear not ; he bears an honourable mind,
    And will not use a woman lawlessly.

Sil. O Valentine, this I endure for thee !   *Exeunt*

SCENE IV

Another part of the forest

Enter Valentine

Val. How use doth breed a habit in a man !
    This shadowy desert, unfrequented woods,
    I better brook than flourishing peopled towns :
    Here can I sit alone, unseen of any,
    And to the nightingale's complaining notes
    Tune my distresses, and record my woes.
    O thou that dost inhabit in my breast,
    Leave not the mansion so long tenantless,

Lest, growing ruinous, the building fall,
And leave no memory of what it was !　　　　　10
Repair me with thy presence, Silvia ;
Thou gentle nymph, cherish thy forlorn swain !
What halloing and what stir is this to-day ?
These are my mates, that make their wills their law,
Have some unhappy passenger in chase :
They love me well ; yet I have much to do
To keep them from uncivil outrages.
Withdraw thee, Valentine : who 's this comes here ?

Enter Proteus, Silvia, and Julia

Pro. Madam, this service I have done for you,
(Though you respect not aught your servant doth　20
To hazard life, and rescue you from him
That would have forc'd your honour and your love,
Vouchsafe me, for my meed, but one fair look ;
A smaller boon than this I cannot beg,
And less than this, I am sure, you cannot give.
Val. (*aside*) How like a dream is this ! I see and hear ;
Love, lend me patience to forbear awhile.
Sil. O miserable, unhappy that I am !
Pro. Unhappy were you, madam, ere I came ;
But by my coming I have made you happy.　　　30
Sil. By thy approach thou mak'st me most unhappy.

Jul. (*aside*) And me, when he approacheth to your
　　　　presence.

Sil. Had I been seized by a hungry lion,
　　I would have been a breakfast to the beast,
　　Rather than have false Proteus rescue me.
　　O, Heaven be judge how I love Valentine,
　　Whose life 's as tender to me as my soul !
　　And full as much (for more there cannot be)
　　I do detest false perjur'd Proteus :
　　Therefore be gone, solicit me no more.　　　　　　40

Pro. What dangerous action, stood it next to death,
　　Would I not undergo, for one calm look !
　　O, 'tis the curse in love, and still approv'd,
　　When women cannot love where they 're belov'd !

Sil. When Proteus cannot love where he 's belov'd.
　　Read over Julia's heart, (thy first, best love)
　　For whose dear sake thou didst then rend thy faith　　†
　　Into a thousand oaths ; and all those oaths
　　Descended into perjury, to love me.
　　Thou hast no faith left now, unless thou 'dst two,　　50
　　And that 's far worse than none ; better have none
　　Than plural faith, which is too much by one :
　　Thou counterfeit to thy true friend !

Pro.　　　　　　　　　　　　　In love
　　Who respects friend ?

93

Sil.   All men but Proteus.

Pro. Nay, if the gentle spirit of moving words
       Can no way change you to a milder form,
       I 'll woo you like a soldier, at arms' end,
       And love you 'gainst the nature of love,—force ye.

Sil. O heaven !

Pro.   I 'll force thee yield to my desire.

Val. Ruffian, let go that rude uncivil touch,   60
       Thou friend of an ill fashion !

Pro.   Valentine !

Val. Thou common friend, that 's without faith or love,
       For such is a friend now ; treacherous man !
       Thou hast beguil'd my hopes ; nought but mine eye
       Could have persuaded me : now I dare not say
       I have one friend alive ; thou wouldst disprove me.
       Who should be trusted, when one's own right hand
       Is perjur'd to the bosom ? Proteus,
       I am sorry I must never trust thee more,
       But count the world a stranger for thy sake.   70
       The private wound is deepest : O time, most
          accurst,
       'Mongst all foes that a friend should be the worst !

Pro. My shame and guilt confounds me.
       Forgive me, Valentine : if hearty sorrow
       Be a sufficient ransom for offence,

94

I tender 't here ; I do as truly suffer
As e'er I did commit.

Val.   Then I am paid ;
And once again I do receive thee honest ;
Who by repentance is not satisfied
Is nor of heaven, nor earth ; for these are pleas'd.   80
By penitence the Eternal's wrath 's appeas'd :
And, that my love may appear plain and free,
All that was mine in Silvia I give thee.

Jul. O me unhappy !   *Swoons*

Pro. Look to the boy.

Val. Why, boy ? why, wag, how now ? what 's the
matter ?   Look up ; speak.

Jul. O good sir, my master charg'd me to deliver a ring
to Madam Silvia, which, out of my neglect, was
never done.   90

Pro. Where is that ring, boy ?

Jul.   Here 'tis ; this is it.

Pro. How ? let me see :
Why, this is the ring I gave to Julia.

Jul. O, cry you mercy, sir, I have mistook :
This is the ring you sent to Silvia.

Pro. But how cam'st thou by this ring ?   At my
depart
I gave this unto Julia.

Jul. And Julia herself did give it me ;
 And Julia herself hath brought it hither.

Pro. How ? Julia ?   100

Jul. Behold her, that gave aim to all thy oaths,
 And entertain'd 'em deeply in her heart.
 How oft hast thou with perjury cleft the root !
 O Proteus, let this habit make thee blush !
 Be thou asham'd that I have took upon me
 Such an immodest raiment, if shame live
 In a disguise of love :
 It is the lesser blot, modesty finds,
 Women to change their shapes than men their minds.

Pro. Than men their minds ? 'tis true. O heaven, were
  man   110
 But constant, he were perfect ! That one error
 Fills him with faults ; makes him run through all the
  sins :
 Inconstancy falls off ere it begins.
 What is in Silvia's face, but I may spy
 More fresh in Julia's with a constant eye ?

Val. Come, come, a hand from either :
 Let me be blest to make this happy close ;
 'Twere pity two such friends should be long foes.

Pro. Bear witness, Heaven, I have my wish for ever.

Jul. And I mine.   120

Enter Outlaws, with Duke and Thurio

Outlaws. A prize, a prize, a prize!

Val. Forbear, forbear, I say! it is my lord the duke.
 Your Grace is welcome to a man disgrac'd,
 Banished Valentine.

Du.   Sir Valentine?

Thu. Yonder is Silvia; and Silvia's mine.

Val. Thurio, give back; or else embrace thy death;
 Come not within the measure of my wrath;
 Do not name Silvia thine; if once again,
 Verona shall not hold thee. Here she stands:
 Take but possession of her with a touch: 130
 I dare thee but to breathe upon my love.

Thu. Sir Valentine, I care not for her, I:
 I hold him but a fool that will endanger
 His body for a girl that loves him not:
 I claim her not, and therefore she is thine.

Du. The more degenerate and base art thou,
 To make such means for her as thou hast done,
 And leave her on such slight conditions.
 Now, by the honour of my ancestry,
 I do applaud thy spirit, Valentine,   140
 And think thee worthy of an empress' love:
 Know, then, I here forget all former griefs,
 Cancel all grudge, repeal thee home again,

Plead a new state in thy unrival'd merit,
To which I thus subscribe : Sir Valentine,
Thou art a gentleman, and well deriv'd,
Take thou thy Silvia, for thou hast deserv'd her.

Val. I thank your grace ; the gift hath made me happy.
I now beseech you, for your daughter's sake,
To grant one boon that I shall ask of you.   150

Du. I grant it, for thine own, whate'er it be.

Val. These banish'd men, that I have kept withal,
Are men endued with worthy qualities :
Forgive them what they have committed here,
And let them be recall'd from their exile :
They are reformed, civil, full of good,
And fit for great employment, worthy lord.

Du. Thou hast prevail'd, I pardon them and thee :
Dispose of them, as thou know'st their deserts.
Come, let us go, we will include all jars   160
With triumphs, mirth, and rare solemnity.

Val. And, as we walk along, I dare be bold
With our discourse to make your Grace to smile.
What think you of this page, my lord ?

Du. I think the boy hath grace in him ; he blushes.

Val. I warrant you, my lord, more grace than boy.

Du. What mean you by that saying ?

Val. Please you, I 'll tell you as we pass along,

That you will wonder what hath fortuned.
Come, Proteus, 'tis your penance but to hear   170
The story of your loves discovered :
That done, our day of marriage shall be yours,
One feast, one house, one mutual happiness. *Exeunt*

Notes

I. i. 22. *Leander* swam the Hellespoint to his lover Hero.

I. i. 72, 73. The quibble depends on the very similar pronunciation of *sheep* and *ship*.

I. i. 141. Cf. *The Tempest*, I. i. 25-30.

I. ii. 7-20. Cf. *Merchant of Venice*, I. ii. 35-115.

I. ii. 80-97. In these lines there is an elaborate series of puns; a *note* is a note written and also a note of music; *set* is to write and also to set to music or perhaps to 'give the note,' and also to set store by; *burden* is a load and also a refrain; *reach so high* is aspire so much above me in rank and also reach so high a note with my voice; it looks as though *sharp* and *flat*, besides their musical meanings, implied a pin-prick or a pinch and a slap; *mean* is tenor voice and lament; *bass* has a pun on base conduct; and *bid the base* is a phrase from the game of prisoner's base, meaning that one of the players gives the prisoner at the base a chance to escape by persuading the opposite side to chase himself.

I. ii. 83. *Light o' Love*; cf. *Much Ado about Nothing*, III. iv. 38.

I. ii. 98. *babble*; we should perhaps read *bauble*, since, if his copy read *bable*, the compositor might legitimately take it as either.

I. ii. 137. *a month's mind*; this clearly means 'a strong inclination,' but why it does is not satisfactorily explained, and references to 'a mass said a month after death' do not help much.

II. i. 35. *none else would*; understand, I think, 'perceive.'

II. i. 73. *to put on your hose*; there has been much trouble about this. I doubt if it means more than 'you are so much more love-sick than the man you twitted that you can't see to put your hose on, let alone garter them.' It is a feeble joke, but Speed is a feeble joker.

II. iii. 28. *a wood woman*; so Theobald for F's *a would-woman*. *Wood* means ' mad,' but the sense is none too good.

II. iv. 126. *thoughts*; the New Cambridge editors suggest *thongs*.

II. iv. 178. Cf. *Romeo and Juliet*.

II. iv. 192. *Is it mine, or Valentine's praise*; F reads *It is* and the New Cambridge editors state that F also prints a full stop after *mine*, though continuing with lower case *o*. This is certainly not in all copies of F. The line is obviously enough corrupt, but I can see no evidence of a cut. The balance of *mine* and *Valentine's* seems exactly right against the *her* and *my* of the following line. Proteus appears to mean ' Is it my own judgment or Valentine's praise?' We can emend ' to taste.'

II. iv. 205. *her picture*; if this is to be taken at its face value, there has been some serious dislocation or tinkering. The remark would suit exactly if Valentine had shown Proteus Silvia's portrait. Otherwise we must assume that *picture* means just ' outside seen at a casual glance.'

II. vii. 32. *wild ocean*; I hesitate to tamper with the text, but *wild* is almost impossibly inapposite, since the ocean here is the peaceful Elysium. We should probably read *wide* (with Collier) or perhaps (graphically easier) *mild*.

III. i. 153. *Phaethon*; traditionally son of Phœbus and Clymene. There seems to be confusion in his genealogy here, since Merops, king of Cos, was indeed married to Clymene, but not the father of Phaethon. Phaethon tried to drive the horses of the sun, and was killed by being hurled from the chariot when he lost control of them.

III. i. 216. *there is a proclamation* . . .; no doubt there is an almost absurd compression of time here with the text as it stands;

but I doubt whether it bothers an audience, and therefore whether we are justified in assuming that an ' interval-scene ' has been cut.

III. ii. 77-78. *such integrity : For Orpheus' lute*; the awkwardness of the transition is so extreme that we are, I think, justified in assuming an omission (though not necessarily a cut). The expected continuation after *such* is *as* followed by some statement which will introduce the *For* and *Orpheus' lute*.

IV. i. 27. *I kill'd a man*; ' the abridged text gives no reason for Valentine's falsehood ' (New Cambridge). Even if we accept the assumption of abridgement, is there any reason why the full text should have been more explicit? Homicide was likely to appeal more to outlaws as a cause of outlawry than a somewhat ridiculous misfire of an elopement. But what is admittedly rather suspicious (unless it is a touch of irony, to show that Valentine might as well have told the truth) is the cause of the third outlaw's outlawry.

IV. iv. 37. *Silvia*; Warburton read *Julia*, perhaps rightly. On this occasion at least Launce's speeded exit left no time for taking leave.

V. iv. 47-9. The sense is clear; Proteus had expressed his faith in a thousand oaths and all those oaths had been forsworn. Theobald suggested *discandied* for *descended*; *rend* also is suspicious, though not quite impossible.

Glossary

MANY words and phrases in Shakespeare require glossing, not because they are in themselves unfamiliar, but for the opposite reason, that Shakespeare uses in their Elizabethan and unfamiliar sense a large number of words which seem so familiar that there is no incentive to look for them in the glossary. It is hoped that a glossary arranged as below will make it easy to see at a glance what words and phrases in any particular scene require elucidation. A number of phrases are glossed by what seems to be, in their context, the modern equivalent rather than by lexicographical glosses on the words which compose them.

Act First

SCENE I

line
8 SHAPELESS, aimless
17 GRIEVANCE, peril
18 BEADSMAN, one who sings intercessory masses
27 GIVE . . . THE BOOTS, make a fool of
34 HOWEVER, in any case
36 CIRCUMSTANCE, round-about discourse
46 BLOW, bloom
52 FOND, foolish
53 ROAD, harbour

line
84 CIRCUMSTANCE, detailed proof
96 LAC'D MUTTON, prostitute (wearing laced bodice)
100 POUND, put in enclosure for strayed animals
108 NODDY, simpleton
131 STONES, *with pun on sense of testicles*
135 TESTERNED, ' tipped '
143 DEIGN, deign to look at
144 POST, messenger

SCENE II

4 RESORT, company resorting to me

17 PASSING, surpassing
19 CENSURE, express opinions

Act I   Sc. ii—*continued*

line

41 BROKER, go-between

51 IT WERE A SHAME, it would shame me

58 TESTY, fractious

68 STOMACH, *pun on* (i) appetite, (ii) anger

94 DESCANT, variations

line

99 COIL, ado

102 MAKES IT STRANGE, pretends anger

116 SEARCH, probe

126 SITH, since

139 WINK, have eyes shut

SCENE III

1 SAD, serious

15 IMPEACHMENT, disgrace

18 HAMMERING, repeatedly pondering

32 IN EYE, within reach of

44 BREAK WITH, disclose intentions to

63 SORTED, in consort with

64 MUSE, wonder

69 EXHIBITION, maintenance

71 EXCUSE IT NOT, make no excuses about it

83 EXCEPTED, run contrary

Act Second

SCENE I

17 WREATHE, cross

23 PULING, whining

26 PRESENTLY, immediately

38 URINAL, test-tube for testing urine

46 HARD-FAVOUR'D, plain

78 SWING'D, whipped

80 AFFECTED TO, loving

81 SET, seated

89 MOTION, marionette

101 CLERKLY, like a scholar

106 STEAD, benefit

107 PLEASE YOU, if it pleases you

149 NONE, *sc. earnest (in sense of reward)*

159 IN PRINT, plainly

SCENE III

35 POST, hasten

GLOSSARY

SCENE IV

SCENE V

SCENE VI

SCENE VII

Act Third

SCENE I

line		line	
4	DISCOVER, reveal	164	EXPEDITION, haste
18	DRIFT, purpose	177	SHADOW, image
21	TIMELESS, untimely	182	ESSENCE, being
28	JEALOUS, suspicious		LEAVE, cease
34	SUGGESTED, tempted	251	EXPOSTULATE, expatiate
42	PRESENTLY, at once	268	GOSSIPS, godparents (*i.e.* for an
45	AIMED AT, guessed		illegitimate child)
47	PRETENCE, scheme	287	JOLT-HEAD, numskull
82	AFFECT, am fond of	303	STOCK, dowry
	NICE, fastidious	309	SET THE WORLD ON WHEELS, 'let
84	TO, as		things slide'
113	LETS, hinders	321	HATH A SWEET MOUTH, is wanton
115	SHELVING, overhanging	329	PROUD, (i) *modern sense*, (ii) hot-
116	APPARENT, manifest		blooded
117	QUAINTLY, cunningly	334	CURST, shrewish
121	BLOOD, spirit	367	GO, *Launce in next line takes it*
138	ENGINE, instrument		*in sense of* 'walk'
143	SENSELESS, without perception		

SCENE II

line		line	
17	CONCEIT, opinion	67	SHARP, keen
19	BETTER, readier	68	LIME, bird-lime
36	CIRCUMSTANCE, deliberation	70	SERVICEABLE VOWS, vows of service
41	VERY, true	77	DISCOVER, reveal
44	IS INDIFFERENT, counts neither	84	CONSORT, part-music
	way	85	DUMP, sad tune
52	RAVEL, become entangled	86	GRIEVANCE, grieving
53	BOTTOM, wind (*the* 'bottom' *was*	87	INHERIT, secure
	the core of the skein)	92	SORT, look out
56	THIS KIND, an affair of this kind	94	GIVE THE ONSET TO, put into
62	LUMPISH, in the dumps		practice

Act Fourth

SCENE I

SCENE II

SCENE III

SCENE IV

Act Fifth

SCENE I

line
6 EXPEDITION, haste

line
12 RECOVER, reach

SCENE II

14 WINK, shut eyes
23 DERIV'D, descended (*in both senses*)

28 OWE, own

SCENE III

4 LEARN'D, taught

SCENE IV

43 APPROV'D, confirmed
101 GAVE AIM TO, was object of
104 HABIT, garment
143 REPEAL, recall

160 INCLUDE, cover up
    JARS, discords
169 FORTUNED, happened
171 DISCOVERED, revealed